ideals

DANNON® YOGURT COOKBOOK

We suggest that you use lowfat yogurt in preparing these delicious recipes. More and more studies have recommended lowfat foods, including recent research by the US Government and the National Academy of Sciences. The "Dietary Guidelines for Americans," issued by the Departments of Agriculture and of Health, Education and Welfare call for cutting down on fat and recommend lowfat yogurt as one of the foods to choose from every day!

Ideals Publishing Corp.
Milwaukee, Wisconsin

Contents

Cover recipes:
Moroccan Shish Kebab, page 31
Salad with Vinaigrette Sauce, page 24

Pictured opposite:
Baked Yogurt Chicken, page 34
California Salad, page 21
Raspberry-Cranberry Punch, page 6
Citrus Delight, page 8
Boysenberry Frappé, page 8

ISBN 0-8249-3010-X

Copyright © MCMLXXXII by The Dannon Company
All rights reserved.
Printed and bound in the United States of America

Published by Ideals Publishing Corporation
11315 Watertown Plank Road
Milwaukee, Wisconsin 53226
Published simultaneously in Canada

A very special thank you to The Dannon Company for their cooperation and help
in supplying recipes from their files. All recipes were prepared using Dannon
Yogurt.

®The Dannon Logo is a Trademark of The Dannon Company,
Ideals Publishing Corporation, Licensee.

Yogurt Basics

What could someone named Dr. Ilya Metchnikoff, winner of the Nobel Prize for Physics in 1908, possibly have to do with sweeping changes being made today to home and restaurant menus across the nation? A lot. But let's go back more than 70 years.

In 1910, Metchnikoff was head of the famed Pasteur Institute in Paris, and was deeply involved in a study of premature aging in humans. Investigating records of human longevity, he discovered that in the country of Bulgaria, for every thousand deaths recorded, an average of four were of people over the age of 100. He also discovered that yogurt was a major part of the Bulgarian diet, and became convinced that this was the secret to their long life. Yogurt is a cultured milk product similar to custard in texture. Metchnikoff isolated the friendly agents that turn milk into yogurt, and set the stage for the beginning of commercial yogurt production. Yogurt enjoyed widespread popularity in Europe prior to its beginnings in America.

When The Dannon Company, now the largest producer of lowfat yogurt in this country, introduced its product here in the early 1940's yogurt did not receive immediate public acceptance. In fact, it was greeted by little more than puzzlement. But when Dannon added fruit preserves to yogurt in 1947, consumer interest increased and the first step was taken toward what would be a yogurt revolution in America.

Recent industry studies have revealed that yogurt is the fastest growing dairy category in terms of consumption. One look in the dairy case at most supermarkets and suspicions are confirmed; America is hooked on yogurt! Once identified as "sour milk with a college education," yogurt is making history. It has gained such broad consumer acceptance that yogurt is now considered a general convenience food.

Yogurt may be a quick and tasty snack, but nutritionists, home economists, and most of all, the yogurt producers, take it very seriously. The nutritional benefits of lowfat yogurt, such as Dannon, are found in vitamins, minerals and other food values. A good source of protein, calcium and riboflavin, yogurt offers exceptional food value with reasonable calorie content.

Americans are expected to eat their way through 1.5 billion 8-ounce containers of yogurt this year. That's a lot of yogurt, and a lot of incentive for the dairy industry. Juan E. Metzger, who guided Dannon during most of its first 40 years, says "The surface has only been scratched. One of every four or five Americans eats yogurt, and only one in ten does so on a regular basis. But we are establishing a broad base among younger consumers, particularly college students, and that should mean steady growth in the years ahead."

In the 1960's large dairy companies competed for the yogurt consumer's attention and increased recognition of the product on a national level. Concurrently, the popularization of health foods and the dawn of the age of consumerism arrived. Yogurt's appeal as a light, healthy, highly-nutritious, and convenient food value proved the crowning touch, assuring yogurt a permanent place in the American diet.

But who exactly is eating yogurt these days? Everyone from school teachers and infants to business executives and taxi drivers. We eat hundreds of millions of pounds of yogurt annually. Yogurt has found its way into corporate cafeterias as well as home refrigerators, and has begun to appear on breakfast, luncheon and dessert menus. Yogurt can be substituted for sour cream, buttermilk or mayonnaise in many recipes at a lesser calorie count, without sacrificing any flavor.

Now that yogurt has gained broad acceptance on its own, creative cooks are developing interesting ways that it can enhance other foods, and served not just as a snack but incorporated into any meal. Homemakers and professional chefs alike have discovered that yogurt is a versatile food that can be served in an array of styles, and combined with other foods to make imaginative appetizers, salads, desserts, entrees and beverages. From soup to salad dressings to tasty frozen yogurt, the immigrant "sour milk with a college education" has become a part of our lives . . . and cuisine.

Enjoy using this delightful collection of delicious recipes . . . and put a little yogurt into your life!

FLAVORFUL ADDITIONS TO 8 OUNCES OF PLAIN LOWFAT YOGURT:

½ cup sliced fruit (strawberries, cherries, bananas, peaches, etc.)

¼ cup chopped nuts

¼ cup chopped dried fruit

¼ cup sliced pineapple,
1 tablespoon shredded coconut

1 tablespoon raisins,
1 tablespoon applesauce,
dash cinnamon, dash nutmeg

1 tablespoon grated carrot,
1 tablespoon diced celery,
1 tablespoon diced radishes,
1 tablespoon diced green pepper,
dash garlic salt, dash onion powder

1 tablespoon honey

1 tablespoon canned nectar (peach, apricot, pear, etc.)

1 tablespoon preserves or marmalade

1 tablespoon shredded coconut

1 tablespoon applesauce,
dash cinnamon

1 tablespoon liqueur (creme de menthe, creme de cacao, curacao, etc.)

2 teaspoons frozen fruit juice concentrate (orange, grape, pineapple, etc.)

1 teaspoon sweetened soft drink mix

1 teaspoon flavored gelatin

1 teaspoon instant cocoa powder

1 teaspoon pudding mix

1 teaspoon maple syrup

1 teaspoon sugar, dash fresh lemon or lime juice

1 teaspoon chocolate syrup

Beverages

Raspberry Cooler

Makes 2 servings.

1 8-ounce container raspberry yogurt
½ cup pineapple juice
¼ cup cream of coconut
3 ice cubes
   Shredded coconut for garnish

Combine yogurt, pineapple juice, cream of coconut and ice cubes in blender. Pour into 2 glasses; garnish with shredded coconut.

Raspberry-Cranberry Punch

Makes 6 servings.

1 8-ounce container raspberry yogurt
½ cup cranberry juice
½ cup orange juice
1 10-ounce package frozen raspberries
2 ounces cranberry liqueur
   Orange slices for garnish

Combine all ingredients except orange slices in blender; process until completely liquified. Strain into cups. Garnish with orange slices.

Tropical Shake

Makes 1 serving.

1 8-ounce container piña colada yogurt
1 ice cube
1 egg
   Pineapple slice dipped in shredded coconut
   for garnish

Combine all ingredients except pineapple in blender until smooth and frosty. Garnish with pineapple slice.

Mocha Frappé

Makes 1 serving.

1 8-ounce container vanilla yogurt
1 tablespoon instant coffee
1 tablespoon instant chocolate mix
2 ice cubes

Mix ingredients thoroughly in blender. Pour into a tall glass.

Citrus Shake

Makes 6 servings.

1 cup vanilla ice cream
2 8-ounce containers pineapple-orange yogurt
2 cups chilled orange or pineapple juice

Mix all ingredients in blender until smooth.

Coco Blizzard

Makes 2 servings.

½ cup pineapple juice or orange juice
½ cup plain yogurt
½ cup cream of coconut
8 ounces club soda
   Ice cubes

Combine juice, yogurt and cream of coconut in blender; blend at medium speed for 30 seconds. Pour into 2 glasses; add club soda and ice cubes.

Holiday Frost

Makes 4 servings.

1 8-ounce container plain yogurt
¼ cup peach brandy
¼ cup light rum
1 10-ounce package frozen peaches,
   partially thawed
   Ground nutmeg

Combine yogurt, brandy and rum in blender. Add peaches; cover and blend just until smooth. Pour into glasses; sprinkle with nutmeg.

Eggnog

Makes 1 serving.

1 8-ounce container vanilla yogurt
1 egg
2 tablespoons honey
1 ounce brandy or rum, optional
   Nutmeg

Combine yogurt, egg, honey and brandy in blender; cover and blend on high speed about 2 minutes until smooth and frothy. Pour into a tall glass; sprinkle with nutmeg.

Banana Nog Shake

Makes 2 to 3 servings.

2 ripe bananas, cut in chunks
2 eggs
1 8-ounce container plain yogurt
½ cup milk
2 tablespoons honey
1 teaspoon vanilla
3 ice cubes, optional
2 ounces rum, optional

Combine first 6 ingredients in blender until thick and creamy. Add ice cubes and rum if desired; blend well.

Creamy Cranberry Float, page 8
Holiday Frost
Tropical Shake

Beverages

Peachy Cooler

Makes 1 quart.

- 2 cups cold milk
- 1 8-ounce container peach yogurt
- 1 cup chilled canned sliced peaches with syrup
- ¼ teaspoon almond extract

Combine milk, yogurt, peaches and almond extract in blender until smooth. Serve in chilled glasses.

Citrus Delight

Makes 1 serving.

- 1 8-ounce container lemon yogurt
- ¼ cup frozen orange juice concentrate
- 1 fresh peach or 1 large canned peach, sliced
- 3 ice cubes
  Orange slice for garnish

Combine yogurt, orange juice concentrate, peach slices and ice cubes in blender until smooth. Pour into glass; garnish with orange slice.

Boysenberry Frappé

Makes 1¾ cups.

- 1 8-ounce container boysenberry yogurt
- ¾ cup cold milk
- ¼ cup frozen sliced strawberries in syrup, partially thawed
  Sliced strawberries for garnish

Combine yogurt, milk and strawberries in blender until smooth. Serve in chilled glasses. Garnish with strawberry slices.

Creamy Cranberry Float

Makes 6 servings.

- 2 cups chilled cranberry-apple juice
- 1 pint vanilla ice cream, softened
- 2 8-ounce containers orange yogurt
  Crushed ice
  Orange peel twists for garnish

Combine cranberry-apple juice, ice cream and yogurt in blender until smooth. Pour into 6 glasses containing crushed ice. Garnish with an orange peel twist.

Sherbet Shake

Makes 6 servings.

- 2 cups pineapple sherbet
- 2 8-ounce containers apricot yogurt
- 1 cup chilled orange or pineapple juice

Mix ingredients in blender until smooth and frothy.

Strawberry Shake

Makes 4 servings.

- 1½ pints (3 cups) vanilla ice cream
- ¼ cup milk
- 1 8-ounce container strawberry yogurt
  Few drops red food coloring, optional
  Whipped cream for garnish
- 4 fresh strawberries for garnish

Blend ice cream, milk and yogurt in blender until smooth. Add a few drops red food coloring, if desired. Pour into 4 glasses. Garnish with whipped cream and a fresh strawberry.

Strawberry Fizz

Makes 1 serving.

- 1 8-ounce container vanilla yogurt
- 6 fresh strawberries
- 1¼ ounces chilled Perrier water
  Fresh strawberry for garnish

Place yogurt and strawberries in blender, cover and process until smooth. Reduce speed; add Perrier water. Garnish with a fresh strawberry.

Apple Yogurt Shake

Makes 4 cups.

- 2 8-ounce containers plain yogurt
- 2 apples, peeled and quartered
- ¾ cup apple juice
- 2 teaspoons lemon juice
- 2 teaspoons honey
- 4 to 5 dates, pitted and coarsely chopped

Combine all ingredients in blender. Blend until apples are finely chopped.

Spicy Tomato Quencher

Makes 4 servings.

- 3 cups tomato juice
- 1 8-ounce container plain yogurt
- 1 teaspoon Worcestershire sauce
- 1 teaspoon lemon juice
- 1 to 2 drops Tabasco sauce
  Dash celery salt
  Dash pepper
  Ice
  Lime slices

Combine tomato juice, yogurt, Worcestershire sauce, lemon juice, Tabasco sauce, celery salt and pepper in a blender; cover and blend on medium speed about 2 minutes until smooth. Pour into 4 tall glasses over ice. Garnish with lime slices.

Snappy Vegetable Dip

Makes 2½ cups.

 2 8-ounce containers plain yogurt
⅓ cup catsup
½ teaspoon Worcestershire sauce
 1 envelope (yield 1 pint) ranch-style salad
    dressing mix
½ teaspoon instant minced onion
⅛ teaspoon garlic salt
 3 to 4 drops Tabasco sauce

Combine all ingredients in small bowl; blend well. Chill at least 1 hour.

Shrimp Spread

Makes 2½ cups.

 2 4½-ounce cans cleaned broken shrimp, drained
    and chopped
 1 8-ounce container plain yogurt
 2 tablespoons mayonnaise
 2 tablespoons minced onion
 2 tablespoons minced green pepper
 2 tablespoons minced celery
 2 tablespoons minced stuffed green olives
¼ teaspoon soy sauce
    Dash Tabasco sauce
    Salt and pepper to taste

Mix all ingredients together until well blended. Chill. Serve with crackers or use as a filling for finger sandwiches or celery.

Guacamole

Makes 3 cups.

 3 ripe avocados
 1 small onion, grated
 1 teaspoon chili powder
 1 teaspoon Tabasco sauce
½ teaspoon salt
    Dash pepper
 2 medium, ripe tomatoes, peeled, deseeded and
    chopped
 1 8-ounce container plain yogurt
 1 teaspoon lemon juice
    Tortilla chips

Cut avocados in half lengthwise; peel and remove seeds. Mash in a medium bowl. Stir in onion, chili powder, Tabasco, salt, pepper and tomatoes; mix until smooth. Stir yogurt until creamy. Add to avocado mixture with lemon juice; blend well. Refrigerate 2 hours. Serve with tortilla chips.

Clam Dip

Makes approximately 3 cups.

 1 7-ounce can minced clams, drained, reserve
    1 tablespoon liquid
 2 8-ounce containers plain yogurt
¼ teaspoon Worcestershire sauce
 2 drops Tabasco sauce
¼ teaspoon salt
½ teaspoon onion powder
    Raw vegetables

Combine all ingredients, except raw vegetables, in blender until smooth. Chill. Serve with raw vegetables.

Bacon and Horseradish Dip

Makes 2 cups.

½ cup crumbled cooked bacon
 1 tablespoon horseradish
 1 8-ounce container plain yogurt
 1 tablespoon minced onion
 1 tablespoon minced parsley
 6 ounces cream cheese, softened

Blend all ingredients together thoroughly with a fork. Chill to thicken.

Tropical Dip

Makes 2½ cups.

 2 8-ounce containers piña colada yogurt
10 small macaroons, crushed
 1 large pineapple
    Sliced kiwi
    Sliced papaya
    Seedless grapes
    Sliced peaches
    Assorted berries

Stir yogurt until creamy in a medium bowl. Blend in macaroon pieces. Chill several hours. Slice top off pineapple, about 1 inch below bottom of leaves; hollow out center, reserving shell. Cut pineapple fruit into chunks; remove core. Fill shell with yogurt mixture; place in center of a large platter. Arrange pineapple chunks, kiwi, papaya, grapes, peaches and berries around pineapple shell.

Cheesy Artichoke Appetizers

Makes 12 servings.

1 small onion, minced
1 clove garlic, crushed
Vegetable oil
1 14-ounce can artichoke hearts, drained and diced
4 eggs, lightly beaten
¼ cup bread crumbs
½ pound Cheddar cheese, grated
½ cup plain yogurt
2 tablespoons minced parsley
Salt and pepper to taste
Dash Worcestershire sauce

Preheat oven to 325°. Sauté onion and garlic in a few teaspoons oil in a skillet until soft. Combine artichokes with eggs; add onion mixture and remaining ingredients. Pour mixture into a buttered 7 x 11-inch baking dish. Bake 30 minutes or until knife inserted in center comes out clean. Allow to cool slightly; cut into squares.

Curried Vegetable Spread

Makes 6 servings.

2 tablespoons peanut oil
1 medium onion, minced
1 clove garlic, crushed
1 teaspoon curry powder
1 teaspoon chili powder
2 medium tomatoes, peeled, deseeded and chopped
1 cup peeled, deseeded and diced cucumbers
2 8-ounce containers plain yogurt
2 tablespoons minced fresh coriander *or* parsley
Salt and freshly ground black pepper to taste

Heat oil in a heavy skillet over moderate heat. Sauté onion and garlic until soft but not browned. Add curry powder and chili powder; cook 1 minute, stirring constantly. Remove from heat; add remaining ingredients. Mix gently but thoroughly. Adjust seasonings. Serve with sesame crackers or pumpernickel bread.

Cheese Ball

Makes 1.

3 cups shredded Cheddar cheese
⅓ cup crumbled blue cheese
½ cup plain yogurt
½ teaspoon Worcestershire sauce
¼ cup minced ripe olives
½ cup chopped nuts
¼ cup chopped parsley

Beat Cheddar and blue cheeses together in small bowl until smooth. Add yogurt and Worcestershire sauce; beat until creamy. Stir in olives.

Cover and chill. Shape into ball; roll in nuts and parsley. Chill; allow to come to room temperature before serving.

Marinated Mushrooms

Makes approximately 2 cups.

4 cups water
2 tablespoons salt
1 tablespoon vinegar
1 pound fresh mushrooms, cleaned and trimmed
¼ cup chopped onion
2 tablespoons chopped parsley
2 tablespoons lemon juice
1 tablespoon vinegar
2 teaspoons granulated sugar
¼ teaspoon thyme
¼ teaspoon salt
⅛ teaspoon white pepper
¾ cup plain yogurt

Bring water, 2 tablespoons salt and 1 tablespoon vinegar to a boil in saucepan. Add mushrooms; cover, reduce heat and simmer about 10 minutes. Drain and cool slightly. Combine onion, parsley, lemon juice, 1 tablespoon vinegar, sugar, thyme, ¼ teaspoon salt and pepper in a small bowl; fold in yogurt, then mushrooms. Cover and chill 12 hours or overnight.

Individual Ham Quiches

Makes 4 5-inch quiches.

1 4-ounce can sliced mushrooms, drained
1 cup thinly sliced scallions
2 tablespoons melted butter
4 unbaked, 5-inch pastry shells
⅔ cup shredded Swiss cheese
½ cup chopped cooked ham
¼ teaspoon salt
½ teaspoon white pepper
¼ teaspoon paprika
1 8-ounce container plain yogurt
4 well-beaten eggs

Preheat oven to 400°. Sauté mushrooms and scallions in butter until tender; drain. Spoon into pastry shells; top with cheese and ham. Combine salt, pepper, paprika, yogurt and eggs in a bowl; beat until smooth. Pour mixture over cheese and ham. Bake 20 to 25 minutes or until custard is set and knife inserted into center comes out clean.

Note: May be made in 2 x 3-inch tart shells.

Soups

Hot Yogurt Soup with Meatballs

Makes 4 servings.

- ½ pound lean ground beef or lamb
- 1 small onion, grated
  Salt and freshly ground black pepper to taste
- 3 8-ounce containers plain yogurt
- 1 tablespoon flour
- 3½ cups beef or lamb broth
- ¼ cup uncooked long-grain white rice
- ½ cup drained canned chickpeas, rinsed
- 1½ cups chopped spinach leaves or a combination of spinach and sorrel leaves
- 4 tablespoons finely chopped fresh parsley
- 4 tablespoons finely chopped fresh dill
- 4 tablespoons chopped chives or scallions including tops

Combine meat, onion, salt and pepper in a bowl. Knead until blended. Form mixture into 1-inch balls; set aside. Place yogurt in large kettle. Whisk in flour, then broth until well blended. Bring to a boil over low heat, stirring constantly in one direction. When mixture is slightly thickened, add meatballs and rice; simmer 10 minutes, stirring frequently. Add chickpeas and spinach; simmer an additional 10 minutes or until meatballs and rice are tender. Stir in remaining ingredients, adjust seasoning and simmer 5 minutes.

Potato Soup

Makes 6 to 8 servings.

- 6 slices bacon, cut in ½-inch pieces
- 1 small onion, diced
- 1 green pepper, diced
- 3 cups water
- 1 10-ounce package green beans or mixed vegetables, thawed
- ½ teaspoon dillweed
- 4 chicken bouillon cubes
- 3 medium-sized new white potatoes
- 1 cup milk
- 2 tablespoons cornstarch
- 1 8-ounce container plain yogurt
  Garlic salt and pepper to taste

Cook bacon in a 5-quart Dutch oven over medium heat until crisp. Drain, reserving 3 tablespoons of the drippings in pan. Add onion and green pepper; cook, stirring, until soft. Add water, beans, dillweed and bouillon cubes. Peel potatoes, if desired, and dice; add to pan. Simmer, covered, until potatoes are tender when pierced, about 25 minutes. Add milk. Stir cornstarch into yogurt; stir into soup. Cook, stirring, until hot and thickened. Add garlic salt and pepper. Garnish with reserved bacon.

Mushroom Soup

Makes 6 to 8 servings.

- ¼ cup butter or margarine
- 1 medium onion, chopped
- 6 scallions including tops, thinly sliced
- ¾ pound fresh mushrooms, sliced
- 2 teaspoons paprika
- ¼ cup flour
- 6 cups chicken broth
- 2 egg yolks, lightly beaten
- 1½ cups plain yogurt
- ¼ teaspoon dillweed
  Salt and pepper to taste

Melt butter over medium heat in large saucepan. Add onion, scallions and mushrooms; cook, stirring until soft. Blend in paprika and flour. Gradually add chicken broth; cook, stirring, until thickened. Cover and simmer 30 minutes. Mix egg yolks with yogurt and dill. Stir 1 cup hot soup into egg mixture. Return to saucepan and cook, stirring, over low heat just until thickened; *do not boil*. Season with salt and pepper.

Green Chile Soup

Makes 6 servings.

- 2 tablespoons butter or margarine
- 1 tablespoon oil
- 4 to 5 cloves garlic, finely chopped
- 1 medium onion, chopped
- 2 teaspoons paprika
- 4 cups chicken broth
- 1½ pounds tomatoes, chopped
- 1 4-ounce can diced green chiles
- ¼ teaspoon chili powder
  Salt and pepper to taste
- 2 8-ounce containers plain yogurt
- 4 ounces Jack or Cheddar cheese, shredded
- 1 tablespoon chopped cilantro or parsley

Melt butter in large stock pot; add oil. Sauté garlic until lightly browned. Remove garlic and set aside. Add onion to butter; sauté until soft. Add paprika; sauté 1 minute. Add chicken broth, tomatoes, chiles, chili powder, salt and pepper. Bring to a boil; reduce heat and simmer 20 minutes. Stir in yogurt slowly; heat thoroughly over low heat. Add reserved garlic. Ladle into soup bowls; sprinkle with cheese and cilantro.

Hot Yogurt Soup

Makes 8 servings.

- 1 cup semolina
- 1 cup water
- 1 cup medium barley
- 3 quarts meat broth
- 3 cups finely chopped onion
- ½ cup butter
- 2 tablespoons finely chopped mint
  Salt and pepper to taste
- 4 8-ounce containers plain yogurt

Soak semolina in water for 30 minutes. Soak, wash and drain barley; cook in meat broth 1 hour. Add semolina; cook until thickened. Sauté onion in butter until golden. Add onion, mint, salt and pepper to soup; cook 3 minutes. Stir yogurt well and gradually add to soup. Heat thoroughly.

Shrimp Bisque

Makes 6 servings.

- ¼ cup butter or margarine
- 1 medium onion, minced
- 2 tablespoons minced green pepper
- 2 tablespoons flour
- 2 tablespoons tomato paste
- 2 cups light cream or milk
- ½ teaspoon basil or thyme
  Salt and pepper to taste
- ¾ pound cleaned, cooked shrimp
- 2 8-ounce containers plain yogurt
  Lemon slices and chopped chives for garnish

Melt butter in a saucepan; add onion and green pepper and sauté until tender. Mix in flour, tomato paste and cream; cook over low heat, stirring, until sauce becomes thickened and smooth. Add basil, salt and pepper; cook about 5 minutes. Stir in shrimp and yogurt; heat thoroughly. Serve garnished with lemon slices and chives.

Cream of Carrot Soup

Makes 4 cups.

- ¼ cup butter or margarine
- 8 medium carrots, scraped and sliced
- 3 medium onions, chopped
- 4 cups hot chicken broth or stock
- 1 8-ounce container plain yogurt
- ½ cup light cream
- ¼ cup chopped fresh chives or 2 tablespoons freeze-dried chives

Melt butter in a large frying pan; sauté carrots and onion until onion is tender. Add chicken broth, cover and simmer 1 hour. Puree mixture in blender; pour into a 2-quart saucepan. Add

yogurt and cream; stir until smooth. Keep on low heat until ready to serve; *do not boil.* Serve garnished with chives.

Yogurt-Spinach Soup

Makes 4 servings.

- 1½ cups water
- 1 tablespoon instant chicken bouillon crystals
- 1 10-ounce package frozen spinach, thawed and drained
- 2 8-ounce containers plain yogurt
- ½ teaspoon salt
- ¼ teaspoon pepper
- 1 tablespoon chopped dill
- 1 tablespoon chopped chives
  Lemon slices for garnish

Combine water and crystals in blender; add spinach and blend. Add remaining ingredients, except lemon slices; blend thoroughly. Chill 1 hour. Garnish with lemon slices.

Lemon-Avocado Soup

Makes 4 servings.

- 1 large ripe avocado
- 2 8-ounce containers lemon yogurt
- 1 cup milk
- 3 tablespoons minced scallions
- ½ teaspoon salt
  Fresh mint leaves for garnish

Peel avocado, remove pit and cut into chunks. Combine chunks in blender with yogurt, milk, scallions and salt; blend until smooth. Garnish with mint leaves.

Creamy Borscht

Makes 6 cups.

- 1 16-ounce can sliced beets, with liquid
- 1 teaspoon granulated sugar
- ¼ cup lemon juice
- ¼ cup minced onion
- ½ teaspoon salt
- ¼ teaspoon pepper
- ¼ teaspoon dillweed
- 1 8-ounce container plain yogurt
  Additional yogurt for garnish

Combine all ingredients except yogurt in blender until smooth. Stir in 8-ounces of yogurt; chill thoroughly. Serve cold; garnish each serving with 1 tablespoon of yogurt.

Curried Tomato Soup

Makes 4 to 6 servings.

- 1 8-ounce can tomato sauce
- 4 scallions including tops, minced
- 1 teaspoon grated lemon peel
- 1 teaspoon curry powder or to taste
- ½ teaspoon basil
- 1 cup chicken broth
- 1 8-ounce container plain yogurt
  Salt to taste
  Additional yogurt for garnish

Bring all ingredients except yogurt and salt to boil in saucepan; cool. Combine mixture with 8 ounces yogurt in blender. Season with salt. Chill; serve topped with a dollop of yogurt.

Frosty Cherry Soup

Makes 2¼ quarts.

- 3 cups cold water
- ⅔ cup granulated sugar
- 1 cinnamon stick
- 2 16-ounce cans pitted sour red cherries
- 2 tablespoons cornstarch
- 1 cup heavy cream
- 1 8-ounce container plain yogurt
- ½ cup dry red wine

Combine water, sugar and cinnamon stick in a 2-quart saucepan. Bring to a boil; partially cover and simmer over low heat 15 minutes. Drain liquid from cherries into bowl; stir in cornstarch until dissolved. Remove sugar mixture from heat; remove cinnamon stick. Stir cornstarch mixture into sugar mixture with wire whisk. Cook 5 minutes over low heat, stirring frequently. Remove from heat; blend in cream, yogurt and wine. Add cherries. Refrigerate until chilled.

Spicy Plum Soup

Makes 4 to 6 servings.

- 1 16-ounce jar purple plums, pitted, with syrup
- 2 cups cold water
- ½ cup red wine
- 1 teaspoon lemon juice
- 2 teaspoons grated lemon rind
- 3 tablespoons honey
  Pinch ground cloves
  Pinch ground cinnamon
- 2 teaspoons cornstarch
- ½ cup plain yogurt
- 2 teaspoons light brown sugar
- 2 tablespoons grated candied ginger

Combine plums, syrup, water, wine, lemon juice, lemon rind, honey, cloves and cinnamon in sauce-pan; cook over medium heat 10 to 12 minutes. Remove plums from cooking liquid; put through a sieve or puree in blender. Return pureed plums to saucepan. Make a paste with cornstarch and 2 tablespoons plum mixture; gradually stir into remaining plum mixture. Cook over medium heat, stirring constantly, until slightly thickened. Chill thoroughly. Serve in chilled soup bowls. Combine yogurt and brown sugar; mix well. Top each serving of soup with a heaping teaspoon of sweetened yogurt; sprinkle with ginger.

Iced Strawberry Soup

Makes 4 servings.

- 1 quart strawberries, rinsed, dried, hulled and sliced
- 2 tablespoons dry white wine
- ¼ cup confectioners' sugar or to taste
- 2 8-ounce containers plain yogurt

Combine strawberries and wine in blender until smooth. Force mixture through sieve to remove seeds. Return puree to blender; add sugar and yogurt; blend thoroughly. Chill.

Gazpacho

Makes 8 servings.

- ½ teaspoon ground cumin seed
- ½ teaspoon dillweed
  Dash garlic powder
- 1 teaspoon basil
- 1 teaspoon salt
- ¼ teaspoon ground black pepper
- 1 cup chicken broth
- 3 drops Tabasco sauce
- 1 tablespoon olive oil
- 1 tablespoon red vinegar
- 1 tablespoon lemon juice
- ½ cup tomato juice
- ½ cup plain yogurt
- ½ cup sour cream
- 3 cucumbers, peeled and coarsely chopped
- 1 large Spanish onion, chopped
- 3 medium tomatoes, peeled and chopped
- 1 large green pepper, deseeded and chopped
- 1 tablespoon dried parsley
- 1 teaspoon grated lemon rind

Combine all dry ingredients in blender. Add broth, Tabasco sauce, oil, vinegar, lemon juice and tomato juice. Blend until smooth, about 1 minute. Add yogurt and sour cream; blend 20 seconds. Add cucumbers, onion, tomatoes and green pepper; mix 15 seconds. Refrigerate 2 hours. Garnish with parsley and lemon rind.

Salads

Avocado-Citrus Salad with Yogurt Dressing

Makes 6 servings.

- 3 ripe avocados
- 3 naval oranges, peeled and sectioned
  Yogurt Dressing
  Chopped walnuts for garnish

Cut avocados in half and remove pits. Arrange orange sections inside each avocado half. Pour ½ cup Yogurt Dressing over each avocado half. Garnish with chopped walnuts.

Yogurt Dressing

- 3 8-ounce containers plain yogurt
- 1 tablespoon lemon juice
- 1 tablespoon honey

Blend all ingredients thoroughly.

Endive, Orange and Onion Salad with Lemon Dressing

Makes 6 servings.

- 6 cups torn curly endive
- 3 medium oranges, peeled and sectioned
- 1 small red onion, sliced and separated into rings
  Lemon Dressing

Toss endive, orange sections and onion together in salad bowl. Serve with Lemon Dressing.

Lemon Dressing

- 1 tablespoon granulated sugar
- ¼ teaspoon dry mustard
- ⅛ teaspoon white pepper
- 2 teaspoons fresh lemon juice
- 1 8-ounce container plain yogurt

Combine sugar, mustard and pepper. Blend dry ingredients and juice into yogurt; mix until smooth.

Tomato-Zucchini Salad

Makes 4 servings.

- 2 medium zucchini, thinly sliced
- 1 green pepper, chopped
- ¼ cup thinly sliced scallion
- 1 8-ounce container plain yogurt
- ½ teaspoon dillweed
- ½ teaspoon salt
  Freshly ground pepper
- 2 medium tomatoes, cut into wedges

Combine zucchini, green pepper and scallion in bowl. Add yogurt, dillweed, salt and pepper; blend well. Add tomatoes; toss lightly.

Fresh Mushroom Salad

Makes 4 servings.

- 2 cups chilled romaine lettuce, torn into bite-sized pieces
- 4 cups chilled fresh spinach, torn into bite-sized pieces
- 1 cup sliced fresh mushrooms
- 1 cup red onion rings
- 2 tomatoes, cut into wedges

Place all ingredients in serving bowl. Before serving, pour Dressing over salad; toss lightly.

Dressing

- 1 8-ounce container plain yogurt
- ⅓ cup crumbled blue cheese
- 1 teaspoon granulated sugar
- ½ teaspoon salt
- ½ teaspoon celery seed
- ½ teaspoon basil

Combine all ingredients in small bowl; cover and chill 1 hour to blend flavors.

Molded Cranberry-Orange Salad

Makes 6 servings.

- 1 3-ounce package orange-flavored gelatin
- 1½ cups boiling water
- 1 14-ounce jar cranberry-orange relish
- ½ cup thinly sliced water chestnuts
- 1 8-ounce container plain yogurt
  Crisp salad greens

Dissolve gelatin in boiling water. Chill until slightly thickened. Stir in relish and water chestnuts. Fold in yogurt. Pour into 1-quart mold. Chill until firm. Unmold on crisp salad greens.

Nectarine Cucumber Salad

Makes 4 to 5 servings.

- 1 8-ounce container plain yogurt
- 1 tablespoon chopped fresh mint *or* 1 teaspoon dried mint
- ½ teaspoon salt
- ¼ teaspoon granulated sugar
- 1 clove garlic, minced
- 1¼ pounds nectarines, sliced
- 1 cucumber, pared and thinly sliced

Combine yogurt, mint, salt, sugar and garlic; blend well. Place one-third of the nectarines in shallow serving dish; top with one-half of the cucumbers. Spoon one-third of the yogurt mixture over nectarines and cucumbers; repeat layering. Top with nectarines and yogurt mixture. Cover and refrigerate 2 hours.

Tangy Rice Salad

Makes 4 to 6 servings.

- 1 tablespoon vinegar
- 1 teaspoon lemon juice
- 1 tablespoon vegetable oil
- 4 cups hot cooked rice
- 2 teaspoons curry powder *or* to taste
- ¼ teaspoon turmeric
- ¾ cup raisins
- ⅓ cup finely chopped green pepper
- ⅔ cup yogurt
- ⅔ cup mayonnaise
- Lettuce

Sprinkle vinegar, lemon juice and oil over hot rice; mix lightly. Add curry and turmeric; blend. Stir in raisins, green pepper, yogurt and mayonnaise; blend well. Place in 6-cup mold; chill 2 hours. To serve, unmold on lettuce-lined plate.

Cucumber Borani

Makes 2 servings.

- 1 large cucumber, peeled, deseeded and sliced
- Salt
- 1 small onion, sliced
- 1 clove garlic, mashed
- ½ teaspoon chopped fresh mint
- 1 8-ounce container plain yogurt
- Juice of ½ lemon
- Lettuce
- Walnuts

Season cucumber with salt in bowl. Allow to stand 5 minutes. Drain liquid. Add onion, garlic, mint, yogurt and lemon juice; toss. Arrange on lettuce in salad bowls; garnish with walnuts.

Peanutty Apple Salad

Makes 8 servings.

- 3 cups diced red apples, unpeeled
- 1 teaspoon lemon juice
- 1 cup thinly sliced celery
- ½ cup plain yogurt
- 2 tablespoons mayonnaise
- 1 tablespoon granulated sugar
- ½ cup coarsely chopped peanuts
- Crisp lettuce leaves

Sprinkle apples with lemon juice; toss well. Add celery. Blend yogurt, mayonnaise and sugar in small bowl. Fold into apple mixture; chill. Toss peanuts with apple mixture. Place in lettuce-lined serving bowl.

Peachy Coconut Salad

Makes 6 to 8 servings.

- 2 tablespoons lemon juice
- 2 tablespoons water
- ¼ teaspoon almond extract
- 3 cups cubed, unpeeled fresh peaches
- ½ cup chopped pitted dates
- ½ cup broken pecans
- ½ cup shredded unsweetened coconut
- ¼ cup yogurt
- 2 tablespoons honey

Combine lemon juice, water and almond extract in large bowl. Add peaches; toss until peaches are coated. Add dates, pecans and coconut. Blend yogurt and honey until smooth; fold gently into fruit mixture. Chill thoroughly.

Red Cabbage Coleslaw

Makes 6 servings.

- 1 medium head red cabbage, shredded
- 1 medium onion, minced
- 1 green pepper, deseeded and chopped
- 1 carrot, pared and shredded
- ½ cup plain yogurt
- 3 tablespoons lemon juice
- 1½ teaspoons salt
- ¼ teaspoon garlic powder
- ¼ teaspoon lemon pepper

Toss cabbage, onion, green pepper and carrot together in large bowl. Combine yogurt, lemon juice, salt, garlic powder and pepper in small bowl; fold into vegetables. Chill.

Apple Caraway Slaw

Makes 6 to 8 servings.

- 1½ cups chopped unpeeled red apple
- Lemon juice
- 4 cups shredded cabbage
- ½ cup chopped celery

Dip apple in lemon juice. Toss apple, cabbage and celery with Dressing.

Dressing

- 1 tablespoon vinegar
- 1 teaspoon caraway seed
- 1 teaspoon prepared brown mustard
- ½ teaspoon salt
- ⅛ teaspoon garlic salt
- 1 8-ounce container plain yogurt

Combine vinegar, caraway, mustard, salt and garlic salt in small bowl; fold in yogurt. Chill.

Note: For added color use 2 cups shredded red cabbage and 2 cups shredded green cabbage.

Salads

Potato Salad Platter

Makes 6 servings.

- 1½ pounds unpeeled red potatoes, cooked
  - Yogurt-Mustard Dressing
- ½ pound green beans, cooked
- 1 green or red pepper, cut into rings
- 6 raw mushrooms, quartered
  - Parsley

Chill vegetables. Prepare dressing and chill. Just prior to serving, cut potatoes into wedges. Arrange vegetables on platter; drizzle with Yogurt-Mustard Dressing.

Yogurt-Mustard Dressing

Makes approximately 2 cups.

- 2 8-ounce containers plain yogurt
- 1 to 2 tablespoons prepared brown mustard
- 2 tablespoons chopped capers
- 4 scallions, chopped
- 2 teaspoons granulated sugar
- 2 teaspoons dillweed
  - Salt and pepper to taste

Blend all ingredients in small bowl. Chill.

Vegetable Cheese-Nut Salad

Makes 2 to 4 servings.

- 4 cups iceberg or romaine lettuce, torn into bite-sized pieces
- 1 small bunch watercress, trimmed
- 1 small red onion, thinly sliced
- 3 tablespoons lemon juice
  - Salt and pepper to taste
- 1 cup julienne carrots
- 1 cup julienne zucchini
- 1 cup julienne Cheddar cheese
- ½ cup chopped walnuts
- 1 cup chopped peanuts

Combine lettuce, watercress, onion and lemon juice in large bowl; toss lightly. Add salt and pepper. Combine carrots, zucchini and cheese; sprinkle over lettuce mixture. Top with walnuts and peanuts. Serve with Dressing.

Dressing

- ½ cup plain yogurt
- 3 tablespoons mayonnaise
  - Milk
  - Celery salt to taste
  - Dillweed to taste

Blend yogurt and mayonnaise; thin to desired consistency with milk. Season to taste with celery salt and dillweed.

Chicken and Artichoke Salad

Makes 6 servings.

- 3 cups cubed cooked chicken
- 1 8½-ounce can artichoke hearts, drained or
  - 1 9-ounce package frozen artichoke hearts, cooked, drained and cooled
- 12 toasted almonds
- ½ cup plain yogurt
- ½ cup mayonnaise
- 1 tablespoon lemon juice
  - Salt and pepper to taste
  - Lettuce leaves
- 12 black olives

Combine chicken, artichoke hearts and almonds in large bowl. Blend yogurt and mayonnaise together. Add lemon juice, salt and pepper; blend well. Taste and adjust seasoning. Drizzle dressing over chicken mixture; toss gently. Serve in bowl lined with lettuce leaves. Garnish with black olives.

Curried Chicken Salad

Makes 8 servings.

- 1 8-ounce container plain yogurt
- 1 cup mayonnaise
- 1 teaspoon curry powder
- 1 large onion, chopped
- 2 pounds diced cooked chicken
- 1 cup walnuts
- 1 cup raisins
  - Lettuce leaves
  - Chopped parsley

Combine yogurt, mayonnaise and curry powder in large bowl. Add onion, chicken, walnuts and raisins; toss gently. Refrigerate 2 hours. Serve on lettuce leaves; sprinkle with parsley.

Egg Salad-Stuffed Tomatoes

Makes 4 servings.

- 6 hard-cooked eggs, chopped
- ⅓ cup chopped pimiento-stuffed green olives
- ¼ cup chopped celery
- 2 tablespoons chopped onion
- ¼ teaspoon dry mustard
  - Dash pepper
- ½ cup plain yogurt
- 4 tomatoes, pulp scooped out

Combine all ingredients except tomatoes in bowl; stir until blended. Chill. Fill tomatoes or use as sandwich spread.

Salads

Avocado-Shrimp Salad

Makes 4 servings.

- 2 ripe avocados, peeled and diced
- 2 teaspoons lemon juice
- 2 4-ounce cans medium shrimp, rinsed and drained
- ½ cup cucumber chunks
  Parsley or watercress for garnish

Sprinkle avocado with lemon juice. Combine shrimp (reserve 8 shrimp for garnish), avocado and cucumber in bowl; chill. Toss with chilled Yogurt Dressing. Mound on lettuce; top with shrimp and a sprig of parsley or watercress.

Yogurt Dressing

- 1 8-ounce container plain yogurt
- ½ teaspoon granulated sugar
- ½ teaspoon curry powder
- ¼ teaspoon salt
- ⅛ teaspoon ground black pepper
- ⅛ teaspoon onion powder
- ⅛ teaspoon celery salt
- ⅛ teaspoon paprika
  Dash garlic powder
- ¼ cup chopped onion or 1 tablespoon dried onion flakes

Combine all ingredients in small bowl; blend well. Chill and toss with shrimp mixture.

Note: Small fresh cooked shrimp can be substituted for the canned shrimp.

Taco Salad

Makes 4 servings.

- 1 pound ground beef
  Salt and pepper to taste
- 1 head iceberg lettuce, torn into bite-sized pieces
- 1 avocado, peeled and cut in small pieces
- 1 medium onion, chopped
- 2 medium tomatoes, peeled and chopped
- 1 17-ounce can kidney beans, drained
- 2 cups grated sharp Cheddar cheese
- 1 cup broken tortilla chips

Brown ground beef thoroughly in skillet; add salt and pepper. Remove from heat and cool. Layer lettuce, avocado, onion, tomatoes, kidney beans, cheese and cooked beef in serving bowl. Sprinkle with tortilla chips. Serve with Taco Dressing.

Taco Dressing

- 1 8-ounce container plain yogurt
- ¾ cup chili sauce
- ¼ cup beer

Combine yogurt and chili sauce. Stir in beer.

Cheesy Meat Salad

Makes 6 servings.

- 8 ounces elbow macaroni, cooked
- 1½ cups plain yogurt
- ¼ cup drained sweet pickle relish
- ¼ cup chopped scallion
- ¼ cup diced green pepper
- ½ teaspoon Dijon mustard
- 1½ cups cubed Cheddar cheese
- ½ pound salami or cooked ham, diced
  Parsley

Toss macaroni with yogurt, relish, scallion, green pepper and mustard in bowl. Fold in cheese and salami; chill to blend flavors. Garnish with parsley. Serve with Low-Calorie Salad Dressing.

Low-Calorie Salad Dressing

- 1 8-ounce container plain yogurt
- 3 tablespoons crumbled blue cheese
  Minced onion to taste
  Minced garlic to taste
  Freshly ground black pepper to taste

Combine all ingredients; chill to blend flavors.

Lobster Salad

Makes 6 servings.

- 1 pound frozen lobster tails, cooked and diced
- 3 cups diced cooked red potatoes
- 3 hard-cooked eggs, chopped
- 3 cups sliced cooked green beans
- 1 cup sliced celery
- ½ cup sliced black olives
- ½ cup chopped red onion
- 1 8-ounce container plain yogurt
- 1 teaspoon curry powder
- ½ cup tomato juice
  Salt and pepper to taste
- 3 cups trimmed spinach leaves, washed and drained

Combine first 10 ingredients in bowl. Add salt and pepper to taste. Chill. When ready to serve, line salad bowl with spinach leaves; fill with salad mixture.

Mushroom Chicken Salad

Makes 4 servings.

- 12 ounces fresh mushrooms, cleaned and sliced
- 2 cups cubed cooked chicken
- ½ cup diced celery
- ½ cup plain yogurt
- 2 tablespoons orange juice
- 1 teaspoon crushed tarragon
- 1 teaspoon salt
- ⅛ teaspoon ground black pepper
  Lettuce leaves

Combine mushrooms, chicken and celery in large bowl; set aside. Combine yogurt, orange juice, tarragon, salt and pepper in small bowl. Pour over chicken mixture; mix well. Serve on lettuce.

Potato Salad

Makes 6 servings.

    4 cups diced cooked red potatoes
    ½ cup chopped celery
    ¼ cup chopped green pepper
    ¼ cup chopped onion
    1 tablespoon chopped pimiento
      Dressing
      Hard-cooked egg slices, optional

Combine potatoes, celery, green pepper, onion and pimiento in large bowl. Add Dressing; toss only until blended. Cover and refrigerate 2 hours. Garnish with egg slices, if desired.

Dressing

    1 tablespoon horseradish
    1 teaspoon salt
    ½ teaspoon prepared brown mustard
    1 8-ounce container plain yogurt

Combine horseradish, salt and mustard; gently fold in yogurt.

Tropical Dream

Makes 6 servings.

    3 cups cubed cooked turkey
    ½ cup sliced water chestnuts
    ½ cup diced celery
    ¼ cup sliced scallions
    ½ cup mandarin orange sections
    6 to 12 lettuce leaves
    ½ cup roasted slivered almonds

Combine turkey, water chestnuts, celery and scallions in large bowl; set aside. Prepare Dressing; gently stir into turkey mixture. Add mandarin orange sections. Line 6 individual salad bowls with lettuce leaves. Divide salad evenly among bowls. Sprinkle with almonds.

Dressing

    ½ cup plain yogurt
    ¼ cup mayonnaise
    1 teaspoon frozen orange juice concentrate
    ¼ teaspoon salt

Combine all ingredients in small bowl; blend.

Shrimp-Stuffed Tomatoes

Makes 4 servings.

    4 tomatoes
    1 cup coarsely chopped cooked shrimp
    2 tablespoons finely chopped scallion
    2 tablespoons finely diced green pepper
    ½ cup finely chopped celery
    ½ cup plain yogurt
    2 ounces cream cheese, room temperature
    2 teaspoons white wine
      Salt and pepper to taste
    ½ cup chopped avocado

Slice top off tomatoes. Scoop out pulp. Flute edges if desired; drain upside down on paper towels. Chill. Combine shrimp, scallion, green pepper and celery in bowl. Blend yogurt, cream cheese and wine together in bowl; add to shrimp mixture. Add salt and pepper to taste. Chill. Add avocado just before serving; fill tomatoes.

Bartletts Neufchatel

Makes 4 servings.

    4 fresh Bartlett pears, pared, cored and halved
      Lemon juice
    2 3-ounce packages Neufchatel cheese
    ¼ cup minced parsley
    ¼ cup chopped scallion
    ¼ teaspoon crushed tarragon
    ¼ teaspoon crushed thyme
      Curly endive or iceberg lettuce
    ½ cup plain yogurt mixed with ½ teaspoon curry powder and ½ teaspoon onion salt

Brush pears with lemon juice. Blend cheese, parsley, scallion and herbs in bowl. Spoon cheese mixture into pear halves. Tear endive into pieces; place on serving platter. Arrange pears on greens. Pour yogurt mixture over all.

California Salad

Makes 6 to 8 servings.

    3 6-ounce jars marinated artichoke hearts
    ⅔ cup plain yogurt
    1 teaspoon salt
      Dash pepper
    2 teaspoons granulated sugar
    1 medium head iceberg lettuce, torn into bite-sized pieces
    3 tomatoes, cut into wedges
    ½ medium cantaloupe, peeled and diced

Drain liquid from artichokes into small bowl; blend in yogurt and seasonings. Place lettuce, tomatoes, artichoke hearts and cantaloupe in salad bowl. Pour dressing over salad; toss gently.

Salads

Waldorf Wheel

Makes 12 servings.

 1 6-ounce package strawberry-flavored gelatin
 2 cups boiling water
 1½ cups cold water
 2 medium red apples, diced
 ½ cup diced celery
 ¼ cup chopped walnuts
 2 8-ounce containers lemon yogurt
 1 tablespoon brown sugar
 ¼ teaspoon salt
 ¼ teaspoon cinnamon
   Crisp salad greens

Dissolve gelatin in boiling water. Add cold water; chill until thickened. Stir in apples, celery and walnuts; pour into 6-cup ring mold. Chill until firm, about 4 hours. Combine yogurt, sugar, salt and cinnamon in bowl; chill. Unmold gelatin ring on greens. Serve with yogurt mixture.

Blueberry Fruit Salad

Makes 6 to 8 servings.

 1 cup fresh blueberries
 1 small banana, sliced
 1 cup sliced strawberries
 1 peach, sliced
 1 cup halved seedless grapes
 2 cups cubed watermelon
 ¼ cup orange juice
 ⅓ cup mayonnaise
 ¼ cup plain yogurt
 1 tablespoon honey
 ¼ teaspoon ground ginger

Combine first 6 ingredients and 2 tablespoons of orange juice in bowl; toss gently. Chill. Stir remaining orange juice, mayonnaise, yogurt, honey and ginger together in a separate bowl; chill. Just prior to serving, pour dressing over fruit.

Creme de Menthe Salad Ring

Makes 6 to 8 servings.

 1 3-ounce package lime-flavored gelatin
 ¾ cup boiling water
 1 8¼-ounce can crushed pineapple, drained, reserve juice
 3 tablespoons creme de menthe liqueur
 ½ cup sour cream
 1 cup diced pears, fresh or canned
   Lime slices

Dissolve gelatin in boiling water. Combine pineapple juice, creme de menthe and enough water to equal ¾ cup liquid; add to gelatin. Chill to thicken. Add sour cream; beat until light and creamy. Fold in pineapple and pears. Pour mixture into greased 4-cup ring mold; chill until set. Unmold and pour Dressing into center of ring. Garnish with lime slices.

Dressing

 1 8-ounce container plain yogurt
 1 cup sour cream
 2 teaspoons fresh lime juice

Combine yogurt, sour cream and lime juice in small bowl; blend well.

Western Salad

Makes 12 servings.

 2 tablespoons butter
 1 clove garlic, crushed
 1 cup plain croutons
 3 quarts chilled romaine lettuce, torn into bite-sized pieces
 ¼ cup grated Parmesan cheese

Prepare Dressing. Melt butter in small saucepan; add garlic. Let stand 1 hour. Sauté croutons lightly in garlic butter. Place romaine in chilled salad bowl. Pour on Dressing; sprinkle with Parmesan cheese. Toss to coat romaine evenly with Dressing. Add croutons.

Dressing

 1 8-ounce container plain yogurt
 1½ teaspoons ranch-style dressing mix
 ¼ cup crumbled blue cheese

Combine yogurt, dressing mix and blue cheese. Cover and chill 1 hour to blend flavors.

Spinach and Yogurt

Makes 4 servings.

 3 tablespoons olive oil
 1 small onion, finely chopped
 1 pound spinach, trimmed, washed, coarsely chopped, cooked and drained
 1 8-ounce container plain yogurt
 1 clove garlic, crushed
 ½ teaspoon crushed dried mint
   Salt and freshly ground black pepper to taste
 2 tablespoons finely chopped toasted walnuts

Heat oil over medium heat in heavy skillet. Add onion; sauté until golden, stirring frequently. Add spinach and sauté a few minutes. Remove from heat. Combine yogurt, garlic, mint, salt and pepper in large bowl until well blended. Gradually stir in spinach mixture; blend thoroughly. Taste and adjust seasoning. Transfer to serving bowl, cover and chill 2 hours. Serve sprinkled with walnuts.

Salad Dressings

Yogurt French Dressing

Makes approximately 1¼ cups.

- 1 8-ounce container plain yogurt, chilled
- 2 tablespoons olive oil
- 2 tablespoons freshly squeezed and strained lemon juice *or* to taste
- Salt and freshly ground white pepper to taste

Combine all ingredients in small bowl. Beat until thoroughly blended. Taste and adjust seasoning.

Note: Lime juice or wine vinegar may be substituted for lemon juice.

Variations:

Garlic Yogurt French Dressing: Add 1 medium clove garlic, crushed.

Onion Yogurt French Dressing: Add 2 tablespoons minced shallots, mild onion *or* scallions.

Herb Yogurt French Dressing: Add minced fresh *or* crushed dried herbs such as basil, dill, chives, parsley, tarragon and oregano, alone or in compatible combinations.

Paprika Yogurt French Dressing: Add ½ teaspoon sweet Hungarian paprika *or* to taste.

Curry Yogurt French Dressing: Add 1 teaspoon curry powder *or* to taste, 2 tablespoons minced scallions and, if desired, 2 tablespoons peeled, minced and deseeded tomato. Very good with seafood, chicken, meats or vegetables.

Egg and Olive Yogurt French Dressing: Add 2 hard-cooked eggs, chopped and 8 pimiento-stuffed green olives, chopped.

Yogurt "Mayonnaise"

Makes approximately 2 cups.

- 2 tablespoons butter
- ¼ cup flour
- 1 cup milk
- 1 egg yolk
- 2 tablespoons lemon juice
- ½ teaspoon dry mustard
- ½ teaspoon salt
- 1 8-ounce container plain yogurt

Melt butter in skillet; stir in flour. Add milk; stir over medium heat until thickened. Remove from heat; beat in egg yolk, lemon juice, mustard and salt. Stir in yogurt. Cool.

Yogurt, Lime and Creme de Menthe Dressing

Makes approximately 1¼ cups.

- 1 8-ounce container plain yogurt
- 3 tablespoons freshly squeezed and strained lime juice *or* to taste
- 1½ tablespoons green creme de menthe liqueur
- 1 sprig mint for garnish

Combine yogurt, lime juice and creme de menthe in a small bowl; blend thoroughly. Cover and chill. Garnish with mint sprig. Serve over fruit.

Variation:

Yogurt, Honey and Creme de Menthe Dressing: Substitute 1 tablespoon honey for the lime juice. Blend and serve as above. Omit mint sprig.

Vinaigrette Sauce

Makes approximately 2¼ cups.

- 2 hard-cooked eggs, finely chopped
- Juice of ½ lemon
- 1 teaspoon grated onion
- 1 tablespoon capers
- 2 tablespoons red wine vinegar
- 1 teaspoon Dijon mustard
- 1 teaspoon chopped tarragon
- 1 gherkin, finely chopped
- Salt and ground pepper to taste
- ½ cup safflower oil
- 1 8-ounce container plain yogurt

Combine eggs, lemon juice, onion, capers, wine vinegar, mustard, tarragon, gherkin, salt and pepper in a bowl; mix well. Blend in safflower oil, a little at a time; add yogurt. Chill.

Best-Ever Yogurt Dressing

Makes approximately 1½ cups.

- 1 8-ounce container plain yogurt
- 3 tablespoons vegetable oil
- 1 tablespoon tarragon white wine vinegar
- 2 teaspoons chopped parsley
- 2 tablespoons grated onion
- ⅛ teaspoon ground oregano
- ½ teaspoon salt
- ¼ teaspoon garlic powder
- ⅛ teaspoon white pepper

Place all ingredients in a blender. Cover and blend on high speed 2 minutes or until smooth and creamy. Refrigerate in an airtight jar at least 2 hours before serving.

Herb Garlic Dressing

Makes approximately 1⅓ cups.

- ⅓ cup mayonnaise
- ¾ teaspoon chopped chives
- ½ teaspoon crushed basil leaves
- ½ teaspoon garlic powder *or* 1 clove garlic, crushed
- ½ teaspoon onion salt
- ¼ teaspoon crushed oregano leaves
- 1 8-ounce container plain yogurt

Mix mayonnaise, chives and seasonings in small bowl. Fold in yogurt. Cover and chill.

Green Goddess Dressing

Makes approximately 2 cups.

- 1 8-ounce container plain yogurt
- 1 cup mayonnaise
- 2 tablespoons lemon juice
- 2 tablespoons chopped scallion
- 2 tablespoons finely chopped parsley
- ½ teaspoon Worcestershire sauce
- ¼ teaspoon garlic salt
  Salt and pepper

Combine all ingredients together. Refrigerate for 1 hour or more to blend flavors. Serve with crisp salad greens.

Cucumber Parsley Dressing

Makes approximately 2 cups.

- ½ cup mayonnaise
- 1 cup peeled, deseeded and chopped cucumber
- 1 cup chopped parsley
- 1 clove garlic, minced
- ½ teaspoon salt
- ⅛ teaspoon ground black pepper
- 1 8-ounce container plain yogurt

Blend first 6 ingredients together. Stir in yogurt. Chill. Serve over green salads or fish salads.

Parsley Sauce

Makes approximately 1¼ cups.

- 1 8-ounce container plain yogurt
- ¼ cup chopped parsley
- 1 tablespoon white vinegar
- ½ teaspoon salt

Combine all ingredients in a bowl. Serve chilled over salad greens, cold ham or cold chicken or heat and serve over hot fish or hot spaghetti.

Chili Sauce

Makes approximately 1½ cups.

- 1 8-ounce container plain yogurt
- 1 small jalapeno pepper, trimmed and deseeded
- 8 sprigs fresh coriander, optional
- 1 garlic clove, minced
  Juice of ½ lime
- ½ teaspoon ground cumin seed
- 1 tablespoon coarsely chopped fresh mint leaves
- 2 scallions, trimmed and chopped
- ¼ cup coarsely chopped fresh arugula leaves, optional

Spoon yogurt into mixing bowl. Do not stir at this point or it will become too thin. Add pepper, coriander, garlic, lime juice, cumin seed and mint to blender. Puree; combine with yogurt. Add scallions and arugula; stir until blended. Serve with grilled meat, salads or raw vegetables.

Piquant Dressing

Makes 1½ cups.

- 1 tablespoon anchovy paste
- 4 sprigs parsley
- 1 teaspoon Worcestershire sauce
- ½ teaspoon dry mustard
- 1 clove garlic, cut in half
- 1 tablespoon snipped chives
- 1½ cups plain yogurt

Combine anchovy paste, parsley, Worcestershire sauce, dry mustard, garlic and chives in blender. Cover; blend on high speed 3 to 5 minutes until smooth. Stir in yogurt. Refrigerate 2 hours. Serve over salad greens or vegetable salads.

Seafood Sauce

Makes approximately 1½ cups.

- ½ bunch watercress
- 1 8-ounce container plain yogurt
- ¼ cup catsup
- 2 teaspoons lemon juice
- 2 teaspoons horseradish
- ½ teaspoon salt
  Lemon wedges for garnish

Snip watercress stems in ⅛-inch lengths; reserve leaves. Combine yogurt, catsup, lemon juice, horseradish and salt. Stir in watercress stems. Chill thoroughly. To serve, cut watercress leaves coarsely; stir lightly into mixture. Serve with cold, cooked shellfish. Garnish with lemon wedges.

Yogurt "Thousand Island Dressing"

Makes approximately 2 cups.

2 8-ounce containers plain yogurt
2 tablespoons chili sauce
1 hard-cooked egg, grated
2 tablespoons chopped dill pickle
Salt to taste

Combine all ingredients in a small bowl. Blend well. Refrigerate at least 2 hours in airtight jar before serving.

Mustard-Horseradish Spread

Makes ½ cup.

½ cup plain yogurt
1 teaspoon prepared mustard
1 teaspoon prepared horseradish
Generous dash of salt

Mix all ingredients just until blended. Serve on sandwiches or with cold meats.

Honey Almond Dressing

Makes 2 cups.

½ cup mayonnaise
½ cup honey
¼ cup slivered almonds
¼ teaspoon almond extract
1 8-ounce container plain yogurt

Stir first 4 ingredients together. Fold in yogurt. Chill. Serve over fruit.

Fruit Salad Dressing

Makes approximately 1½ cups.

1 8-ounce container plain yogurt
⅛ cup fresh orange juice
¼ cup shredded coconut

Mix all ingredients together thoroughly. Serve over fresh fruit salad.

Tangy Dressing

Makes approximately 2½ cups.

2 8-ounce containers plain yogurt
2 tablespoons prepared mustard
2 tablespoons chopped capers
4 scallions, finely chopped
2 teaspoons chopped fresh dill *or*
1 teaspoon dried dillweed
Salt and pepper to taste

Blend all ingredients in a bowl. Chill. Serve with green salads or as a sauce for fish or cold beef.

Versatile Yogurt Dressing

Makes approximately 1 cup.

1 8-ounce container plain yogurt
2 tablespoons sweet pickle relish
½ teaspoon onion powder
½ teaspoon salt
¼ teaspoon dry mustard
2 tablespoons chopped pimiento-stuffed green olives, optional

Combine ingredients; blend well. Use as a spread for sandwiches, as a sauce for cooked fish or as a dressing for fish, poultry or ham salads.

Zesty Dressing

Makes approximately 1½ cups.

1 package ranch-style salad dressing mix
½ cup mayonnaise
1 8-ounce container plain yogurt

Blend salad dressing mix and mayonnaise together; stir in yogurt. Chill. Serve with green salads or baked potatoes.

Olive Dressing

Makes approximately 1⅓ cups.

⅓ cup mayonnaise
2 tablespoons finely chopped pimiento-stuffed olives
2 tablespoons chopped onion
1 tablespoon chopped pimiento
⅛ teaspoon garlic powder
½ teaspoon granulated sugar
1 8-ounce container plain yogurt

Combine mayonnaise, olives, onion, pimiento, garlic powder and sugar in small bowl. Fold in yogurt. Cover and chill until serving time. Serve as a dressing for green salads, as a dip for raw vegetables or as a sandwich spread.

Yogurt-Blue Cheese Dressing

Makes approximately 2½ cups.

⅓ cup mayonnaise
1½ cups plain yogurt
2 tablespoons minced onion
1 tablespoon lemon juice
½ teaspoon salt
¼ cup crumbled blue cheese
Juice of 1 garlic clove
Freshly ground black pepper

Combine all ingredients in jar. Refrigerate.

Clockwise from top:
Tangy Dressing
Green Goddess Dressing, page 25
Yogurt, Lime, Creme de Menthe Dressing, page 24
Honey Almond Dressing

Main Dishes

Gourmet Sea Scallops

Makes 4 to 6 servings.

1½ pounds scallops
1½ cups dry white wine
    Salt and pepper to taste
2 tablespoons vegetable oil
3 tablespoons butter *or* margarine
1 tablespoon all-purpose flour
½ cup milk
1 8-ounce container plain yogurt
½ cup chopped mushrooms
2 tablespoons grated Swiss cheese
2 tablespoons bread crumbs

Combine scallops, wine, salt and pepper in large heavy saucepan; cover. Bring to boil over low heat; simmer gently 5 minutes. Drain and reserve liquid. Remove scallops and chop. Heat oil and 1 tablespoon butter in same saucepan. Add flour, stirring constantly. Gradually add cooking liquid and milk; blend thoroughly. Add yogurt, scallops and mushrooms. Cook 5 minutes, stirring occasionally. Remove from heat; add Swiss cheese. Fill buttered casserole with scallop mixture. Sprinkle with bread crumbs, dot with remaining butter and place under broiler a few minutes until golden.

Shrimp Curry

Makes 4 servings.

4 cups sliced mushrooms
1 cup finely chopped onion
2 garlic cloves, crushed
2 tablespoons butter
4 tomatoes, peeled and chopped
1 tablespoon curry powder
1 teaspoon chili powder
    Salt and pepper to taste
2 pounds shrimp, peeled and deveined
2 tablespoons cornstarch dissolved in
    1 tablespoon water
1 8-ounce container plain yogurt
2 cups cooked rice

Sauté mushrooms, onion and garlic in butter in large skillet 3 to 5 minutes or until tender. Stir in tomatoes and seasonings. Simmer uncovered 10 to 12 minutes, stirring occasionally. Add shrimp, cover and cook 8 minutes or until shrimp are pink. Add cornstarch, stirring until thickened. Remove from heat. Stir in yogurt. Serve over rice.

Lobster Thermidor

Makes 4 to 6 servings.

2 tablespoons butter
¼ cup finely chopped celery
1½ tablespoons all-purpose flour
¼ teaspoon salt
1 cup milk
1 egg, lightly beaten
½ cup plain yogurt, room temperature
2 9-ounce packages frozen lobster tails, cooked and cut into ½-inch pieces
½ cup fresh sliced mushrooms
½ teaspoon grated lemon rind
½ teaspoon prepared mustard
2 tablespoons grated Parmesan cheese
    Hot cooked rice

Preheat oven to 350°. Melt butter in saucepan; add celery and sauté 2 to 3 minutes. Add flour and salt, stirring until blended. Remove from heat; gradually add milk. Return to heat and cook, stirring constantly, until thickened. Cook 2 minutes. Add small amount of hot mixture to egg; return all to saucepan. Cook 1 minute. Stir in yogurt, lobster, mushrooms, lemon rind, mustard and cheese. Heat to serving temperature; *do not boil*. Serve over rice.

Fish Fillets with Spicy Sauce

Makes 6 servings.

2 pounds fillets of sole *or* flounder
2 tablespoons prepared horseradish
2 tablespoons Dijon mustard
2 tablespoons lemon juice
3 tablespoons grated Parmesan cheese
⅓ cup plain yogurt
2 tablespoons butter *or* margarine, melted

Preheat broiler. Arrange fish in single layer in broiler pan. Combine horseradish, mustard, lemon juice, Parmesan cheese and yogurt in small bowl. Add butter; stir until smooth. Spread sauce over fillets. Broil 4 minutes or until fish is tender and sauce is bubbly.

Pocket Sandwiches with Sauce

Makes 4 servings.

- ¼ cup steak sauce
- 1 tablespoon vegetable oil
- 1 tablespoon soy sauce
- 1 tablespoon granulated sugar
- 1 garlic clove, finely chopped
- 1 pound ground beef
- 3 tablespoons dry bread crumbs
- 1 teaspoon salt
- 2 individual pita breads
- ¼ cup onion rings
- ¼ cup green pepper strips
- Yogurt Sauce

Combine steak sauce, vegetable oil, soy sauce, sugar and garlic in small bowl for glaze; set aside. Combine beef, bread crumbs and salt in bowl; mix well. Form beef mixture into 4 patties. Grill 6 inches from heat 10 minutes, brushing frequently with glaze. Turn and grill 5 additional minutes. Cut pita breads in half to form 4 pockets. Place a patty in each pocket. Add onion and green pepper. Serve with Yogurt Sauce.

Yogurt Sauce

Makes ½ cup.

- ½ cup plain yogurt
- 1 tablespoon steak sauce
- 1 tablespoon finely chopped onion
- 1 teaspoon granulated sugar
- Dash salt

Combine all ingredients. Serve on meat patties.

Variation: Add 2 tablespoons rich, mild steak sauce, salt and pepper to 1 pound ground beef. Form into patties. Grill as above. Serve in bread pockets with onion, green pepper and mustard sauce made of ½ cup plain yogurt, 1 teaspoon mild mustard and ½ teaspoon onion salt.

Mexican Beef Casserole

Makes 6 to 8 servings.

- 1 tablespoon vegetable oil
- ½ cup chopped onion
- 2 garlic cloves, minced
- 1 pound lean ground beef
- 1 28-ounce can stewed tomatoes, drained
- 1 package taco seasoning mix
- 1 4-ounce can green chilies, drained and diced
- 1 2½-ounce can black olives, drained and chopped
- 1 16-ounce package cheese-flavored tortilla chips, lightly crushed
- ½ pound mozzarella cheese, shredded
- 2 8-ounce containers plain yogurt
- ½ cup shredded Cheddar cheese

Preheat oven to 350°. Heat oil in large skillet over medium heat. Sauté onion and garlic in oil until translucent. Add meat; cook until browned, stirring frequently. Blend in tomatoes, taco seasoning, chilies and olives; simmer 10 minutes. Grease a 9 x 13-inch baking dish. Layer half of chips over bottom; then meat mixture, mozzarella and yogurt. Top with remaining chips. Bake 30 minutes or until heated thoroughly. Sprinkle with Cheddar cheese; bake until cheese melts. Let stand 5 minutes before serving.

Chuck Steak Hawaiian-Style

Makes 4 to 6 servings.

- 1 8-ounce container plain yogurt
- 3 tablespoons soy sauce
- 1 garlic clove, pressed
- ¼ cup vegetable oil
- 2 pounds 1-inch-thick chuck steak

Combine yogurt, soy sauce and garlic in small bowl. Drizzle oil into mixture, stirring constantly. Pierce both sides of steak with a fork. Place meat in a shallow dish. Pour marinade over steak. Cover and refrigerate 8 to 10 hours. Drain marinade; set aside. Grill or broil steak to desired doneness, brushing frequently with marinade.

Chili Pepper Steak

Makes 4 to 6 servings.

- ¼ cup all-purpose flour
- 1½ teaspoons salt
- ½ teaspoon pepper
- 1 to 1½ pounds 1-inch-thick round steak
- 2 tablespoons butter
- 2 garlic cloves, crushed
- 1 medium onion, sliced
- 1 16-ounce can stewed tomatoes, including liquid
- 1 teaspoon chili powder
- 1 8-ounce container plain yogurt

Combine 2 tablespoons flour, salt and pepper in small bowl. Sprinkle one side of meat with half of flour mixture; pound in. Turn meat over; repeat. Cut into serving-size strips. Melt butter in large ovenproof skillet; brown meat. Stir in garlic, onion, tomatoes and chili powder. Cover. Bake at 350° 1 to 1½ hours or until meat is tender. Transfer meat to warm platter. Combine remaining flour with yogurt in small bowl; add to tomato mixture. Heat until sauce thickens; *do not boil*. Pour over meat.

Curried Lamb with Almonds

Makes 6 to 8 servings.

 ¼ cup butter or margarine
 1 large onion, finely chopped
 2 teaspoons minced fresh ginger or ½ teaspoon
  ground ginger
 1½ teaspoons turmeric
 ¼ teaspoon cayenne pepper
 1 tablespoon flour
 2½ pounds lean boneless lamb shoulder, cut in
  1-inch cubes
 ¾ cup water
 ½ cup raisins
  Salt and pepper to taste
 1½ cups plain yogurt
 ½ cup slivered almonds
  Hot cooked rice

Melt 2 tablespoons butter in large skillet over medium heat; add onion and cook until translucent. Stir in ginger, turmeric, cayenne pepper and flour; cook until bubbly. Transfer to bowl; set aside. Melt remaining butter in skillet over medium heat; add lamb, a few pieces at a time; brown well. Add water, cover, reduce heat, and simmer 1½ hours or until lamb is tender. Stir several times during cooking; add more water if needed. Add reserved onion mixture and raisins to lamb; cook, stirring, until mixture is thickened, approximately 3 minutes. Season to taste with salt and pepper. Add yogurt; cook just until heated—*do not boil.* Garnish with almonds. Serve with hot cooked rice.

Leg of Lamb (Greek-Style)

Makes 8 servings.

 2 garlic cloves, crushed
 ¼ cup lemon juice
 ¼ teaspoon coarsely ground black pepper
 ¼ teaspoon ground or crushed anise seed
 1 8-ounce container plain yogurt
 1 6- to 7-pound leg of lamb, boned, trimmed and
  butterflied

Combine all ingredients except lamb in large, shallow glass baking pan. Add lamb to marinade; turn to coat evenly. Marinate, covered, in refrigerator several hours or overnight. Preheat oven to 500°. Place lamb on rack in shallow baking pan. Roast 30 minutes. Baste with marinade. Turn and roast 15 minutes. Outer thin parts of lamb will be well done. Thick portions will be slightly pink. To serve, slice thinly on diagonal.

Persian Lamb Chops

Makes 6 servings.

 6 to 12 1-inch-thick rib or loin lamb chops
 2 tablespoons lemon juice
  Paprika
  Pepper
  Salt
 1 8-ounce container plain yogurt
 ½ cup finely chopped onion
 1 garlic clove, minced

Place lamb chops in glass baking pan; sprinkle with lemon juice. Let stand 5 minutes. Sprinkle generously with paprika, pepper and salt. Combine yogurt, onion and garlic in small bowl. Pour over lamb. Refrigerate; marinate 8 hours. Broil 3 to 4 inches from source of heat, 5 to 7 minutes on each side, or to desired doneness.

Moroccan Shish Kebab

Makes 6 servings.

 1 8-ounce container plain yogurt
 2 tablespoons lemon juice
 1 teaspoon olive oil
 1 large onion, minced
 ½ cup chopped mint leaves
 2 tablespoons chopped fresh coriander or parsley
  Salt and pepper to taste
 ¼ teaspoon cayenne pepper
 2 pounds boned leg of lamb or beef sirloin,
  cut into cubes
 18 cherry tomatoes
 2 green peppers, cut into chunks
 18 pearl onions, peeled
 18 medium-size mushrooms
  Hot cooked rice

Combine yogurt, lemon juice, olive oil, onion, mint, coriander, salt, pepper and cayenne pepper in large bowl. Add meat to marinade mixture. Turn meat to cover; refrigerate 4 to 5 hours for lamb, overnight for beef. Remove from refrigerator 2 hours before cooking. Just before cooking, arrange meat on skewers alternately with tomatoes, peppers, onions and mushrooms. Place on grill 3 inches above coals which should be red hot but not flaming. Cook 5 minutes on each side, turning skewers to brown meat evenly. Serve with rice.

Main Dishes

Dilly Lamb Stew

Makes 4 to 6 servings.

- 1 tablespoon butter
- 1½ pounds lamb stew meat
- 1 teaspoon salt
- ¾ teaspoon dried dillweed
- 2 cups water
- 4 medium potatoes, peeled and quartered
- 4 carrots, peeled and cut into 2-inch pieces
- 3 ribs celery, cut into 2-inch pieces
- 1 8-ounce container plain yogurt
- 2 tablespoons flour

Melt butter in skillet; add meat and brown. Add salt, dillweed and water; cover and simmer 1 hour or until meat is almost tender. Add potatoes, carrots and celery; simmer 30 minutes or until vegetables are tender. Remove meat and vegetables to warm serving platter. Combine yogurt and flour in small bowl. Add yogurt mixture to liquid in skillet. Cook over low heat, stirring constantly until thickened. Cook 2 additional minutes. Pour gravy over lamb and vegetables.

Island Spareribs

Makes 6 servings.

- 4 to 6 pounds country-style spareribs
- 1 6-ounce can frozen pineapple juice concentrate, thawed
- 1 small onion, minced
- 2 tablespoons soy sauce
- ½ cup plain yogurt

Preheat oven to 350°. Place spareribs in shallow baking dish. Cover with foil; bake 50 minutes. Remove foil; drain fat. Bake an additional 20 minutes or until tender. Combine pineapple concentrate, onion, soy sauce and yogurt in small bowl. Brush ribs with half the mixture. Bake 7 minutes. Turn ribs; brush with remaining mixture. Bake an additional 7 minutes.

Curried Pork Roast

Makes 6 to 8 servings.

- 1 5- to 7-pound loin of pork
- ½ cup plain yogurt
- ¼ cup grated onion
- 1 tablespoon vegetable oil
- ¼ cup curry powder
- 2 teaspoons salt
- 1 teaspoon ground ginger
- ½ teaspoon ground cardamom
  Orange slices, optional
  Watercress, optional

Place pork loin, fat-side up, in large shallow baking pan. Combine remaining ingredients in small bowl. Rub mixture over roast. Cover and refrigerate 24 hours. Preheat oven to 325°. Remove pork from dish; place on rack in shallow roasting pan. Roast 2 to 2½ hours or until meat juices run clear when meat is pierced with a fork. Garnish with orange slices and watercress, if desired.

Persian Pork Chops

Makes 4 servings.

- 1 8-ounce container plain yogurt
- 3 scallions, chopped
- ½ teaspoon salt
- ¼ teaspoon white pepper
- 4 thick center-cut pork chops
- 1 teaspoon butter
- ¼ cup dry white wine
- ½ tablespoon cornstarch
- 1 cup chicken broth

Combine yogurt, scallions, salt and pepper in large bowl. Add pork chops, turning to cover completely with yogurt mixture. Marinate 3 hours at room temperature. Remove chops, scraping off as much yogurt mixture as possible and reserve. Melt butter in skillet; sauté chops until browned. Add wine. Cover and simmer until tender. Remove chops to warm platter. Add yogurt mixture to pan juices. Dissolve cornstarch in chicken broth. Stir into yogurt mixture over low heat until thickened. Pour sauce over chops.

Eminces de Veau

Makes 4 servings.

- 3 tablespoons butter
- 20 ounces thinly sliced veal, cut into strips
- 1 cup sliced fresh mushrooms
- 1 teaspoon chopped shallots
- ½ cup dry vermouth
- 1 cup beef stock
- ¼ cup flour
  Salt and pepper to taste
- 1 8-ounce container plain yogurt
  Noodles *or* rice

Melt 1 tablespoon butter in skillet; sauté veal until golden brown. Set aside and keep warm. In same skillet sauté mushrooms 2 minutes. Add shallots, vermouth and beef stock. Cook until liquid is slightly reduced. Mix remaining butter with flour to make a paste; add to skillet, stirring until sauce thickens. Add salt and pepper; return veal to skillet. Bring to a boil. Remove from heat; stir in yogurt. Serve with noodles.

Polynesian Meatballs

Makes 4 servings.

    1 pound lean beef, ground twice
    1 small onion, grated
    ⅓ cup dry bread crumbs
    1 egg, lightly beaten
    ½ teaspoon curry powder
    ⅛ teaspoon ground ginger
      Salt and freshly ground black pepper to taste
    ⅓ cup all-purpose flour
    1 tablespoon peanut oil
    ¾ cup hot beef broth
    ¼ cup dark rum
    ½ cup plain yogurt, room temperature
    ⅓ cup sour cream, room temperature
    ¼ cup shredded unsweetened coconut
    ¼ cup finely chopped macadamia nuts *or* salted cashews

Combine beef, onion, bread crumbs, egg, curry powder, ginger, salt and pepper in bowl. Knead until thoroughly blended and smooth. Shape mixture into 1½-inch balls. Roll lightly in flour. Heat oil in heavy skillet over moderate heat. Add meatballs; sauté until lightly browned on all sides, adding more oil if necessary. Transfer to plate and keep warm. Add 1 tablespoon flour to skillet drippings; mix well. Add broth and rum. Stir constantly until sauce is slightly thickened. Return meatballs to skillet. Cover and simmer 20 minutes, adding more broth if necessary. Stir in yogurt and sour cream. Taste and adjust seasoning. Heat thoroughly, but *do not boil.* Serve sprinkled with coconut and nuts.

Quiche Lorraine

Makes 6 servings.

    1 9-inch unbaked pastry shell
    1½ cups shredded Swiss cheese
    6 slices bacon, cooked and crumbled
    2 tablespoons thinly sliced scallion including tops
    4 eggs, lightly beaten
    1 8-ounce container plain yogurt
    1 tablespoon cornstarch
    ¾ cup milk
    ½ teaspoon salt
      Dash pepper
    ⅛ teaspoon nutmeg
    2 tablespoons grated Parmesan cheese

Preheat oven to 375°. Sprinkle cheese, bacon and scallion over bottom of pastry shell. Beat eggs, yogurt, cornstarch, milk, salt, pepper and nutmeg together. Pour into pastry shell. Sprinkle with Parmesan cheese. Bake 30 to 35 minutes or until a knife inserted in center comes out clean. Let stand 10 minutes before serving.

Pasta Jardiniere

Makes 6 servings.

    1 pound pasta
    2 tablespoons butter
    2 garlic cloves, minced
    2 tablespoons all-purpose flour
    1 cup chicken stock
    ¼ teaspoon crushed red pepper, optional
    1 cup broccoli flowerets, cooked
    1 cup peas, cooked
    1 small zucchini, sliced and cooked
    ½ cup ricotta
    ½ cup plain yogurt
    3 scallions, minced
    2 tablespoons minced parsley
    2 tablespoons grated Parmesan cheese

Prepare pasta according to package directions. Melt butter in large saucepan over moderate heat; sauté garlic, but *do not* brown. Add flour and cook, stirring, until mixture is bubbly. Add chicken stock and pepper; stir until thickened. Add broccoli, peas and zucchini; heat thoroughly. Remove from heat; set aside. Toss pasta with ricotta and yogurt. Add vegetables; toss. Top with scallions, parsley and Parmesan cheese.

Company Brunch Eggs

Makes 6 servings.

    1 medium onion, minced
    ¼ teaspoon garlic powder
    2 tablespoons vegetable oil
    2 tablespoons tomato paste
    ½ teaspoon oregano
    1½ cups plain yogurt
    ⅓ cup sliced black olives
      Salt and pepper to taste
    6 slices ham *or* Canadian bacon, cooked
    6 thin slices Swiss cheese
    6 large eggs
      Dash paprika
    6 slices bread, toasted

Preheat oven to 350°. Sauté onion and garlic in oil in skillet. Add tomato paste and oregano, stirring well. Blend in yogurt and olives. Add seasoning to taste. Cook over low heat several minutes, stirring constantly until blended. Arrange ham in bottom of shallow baking dish. Place cheese over ham. Break an egg onto each cheese slice; top with yogurt sauce. Sprinkle with paprika. Bake 10 minutes or until eggs are set. Serve on toast.

Main Dishes

Pasta with Italian Ham

Makes 6 servings.

- ½ cup grated Parmesan cheese
- ½ cup plain yogurt
- ⅓ cup dry white wine
- 2 tablespoons butter *or* margarine, melted
- 1 10-ounce package frozen asparagus spears, cooked and drained
- 4 ounces thinly sliced prosciutto *or* very thinly sliced smoked ham, cut in 1-inch strips
- 8 ounces linguini, fettucini, spaghetti *or* other pasta
- Grated Parmesan cheese, optional

Combine ½ cup Parmesan cheese, yogurt, wine and butter in small bowl. Stir in asparagus and prosciutto; set aside. Prepare pasta according to package directions. Drain well. Place pasta on warm serving platter; toss with cheese mixture. Sprinkle with additional Parmesan cheese, if desired. Serve immediately.

Chicken India

Makes 8 servings.

- ½ cup butter *or* margarine
- 5 pounds frying chicken pieces
- 2 cups water
- 2 teaspoons instant chicken broth crystals
- 2 cups diced onion
- 2 cloves garlic, minced
- ¼ cup flour
- 1 tablespoon curry powder
- 2 teaspoons salt
- 1 teaspoon pepper
- 1 teaspoon ground coriander
- 1 teaspoon ground cinnamon
- 1 teaspoon ground ginger
- 1 1-pound can whole tomatoes, drained
- 2 teaspoons grated lime rind
- 2 tablespoons fresh lime juice
- 1 8-ounce container plain yogurt

Melt ¼ cup butter in Dutch oven. Brown chicken pieces; remove to paper toweling. Pour off fat. Add water and broth crystals to pan; bring to boiling. Add chicken; lower heat. Cover and simmer 20 minutes until chicken is tender. Remove chicken to 3-quart ovenproof serving dish. Pour off 2 cups chicken broth (add water, if necessary); set aside. Melt remaining ¼ cup butter; sauté onion and garlic until tender, about 5 minutes. Remove from heat. Combine flour, curry powder, salt, pepper, coriander, cinnamon and ginger. Sprinkle over onion, mixing thoroughly. Gradually stir in reserved chicken broth until mixture is smooth. Add tomatoes; break up slightly with spoon. Bring to boiling; lower heat. Cover and simmer 15 minutes, stirring occasionally. Stir lime rind and juice into sauce with yogurt. Pour over chicken. Turn chicken pieces to coat with sauce. Cool 15 minutes. Cover; refrigerate 2 to 4 hours. Preheat oven to 350°. Stir chicken mixture. Cover; bake 35 minutes. Stir again; bake an additional 40 minutes.

Greek Chicken

Makes 4 to 6 servings.

- 4 whole chicken breasts, boned and split
- ¼ cup lemon juice
- 1 teaspoon salt
- ½ teaspoon pepper
- ¼ cup butter
- 1 small onion, finely chopped
- ¼ cup honey
- ¼ teaspoon nutmeg
- 1½ cups chicken broth
- 1½ cups plain yogurt
- Parsley for garnish

Rub all sides of chicken with lemon juice; season with salt and pepper. Melt butter in large skillet. Sauté chicken breasts until golden brown on both sides. Remove to warm plate. Add onion; sauté until transparent. Stir in honey, nutmeg, broth and yogurt; simmer 5 minutes; *do not boil*. Taste and adjust seasoning. Return chicken to pan; spoon sauce over chicken. Cover and cook over low heat 30 minutes or until chicken is tender. Garnish with parsley.

Baked Yogurt Chicken

Makes 4 servings.

- 1 2½- to 3-pound frying chicken, cut up
- Salt and pepper to taste
- 6 tablespoons butter *or* margarine
- 2 tablespoons all-purpose flour
- 1 tablespoon paprika
- 2 8-ounce containers plain yogurt
- ¼ pound fresh mushrooms, cleaned and sliced
- 2 tablespoons fresh lemon juice
- 2 tablespoons chopped fresh dill *or* parsley

Preheat oven to 325°. Season chicken with salt and pepper. Melt 4 tablespoons of butter in large skillet; sauté chicken until golden brown and place in buttered baking dish. Sprinkle flour and paprika into skillet; cook, stirring, 1 minute. Stir in yogurt; mix well. Pour over chicken. Sauté mushrooms in remaining butter and lemon juice 1 minute; spoon over chicken. Sprinkle with dill. Bake, covered, 1 hour or until tender.

Main Dishes

Chicken Paprikash

Makes 4 servings.

- 1 2½- to 3-pound frying chicken, cut up, skinned and boned, including giblets
  Salt and pepper to taste
- 5 tablespoons sweet Hungarian paprika
- 5 tablespoons shortening
- 1 cup finely chopped onion
- 3 tablespoons tomato puree
- 1 garlic clove, mashed
- 1 to 2 cups chicken stock or water
- 1 medium green pepper, cut into strips
- 1 teaspoon salt
- ½ cup sour cream
- ½ cup yogurt

Slice giblets; season with salt, pepper and 1 tablespoon paprika. Heat 4 tablespoons shortening in large, heavy skillet; add chicken and giblets and sauté over medium heat until meat turns white. Remove chicken, except giblets, and keep warm. Add onion, 2 tablespoons paprika, tomato puree and garlic to skillet; cook over high heat several minutes. Add 1 cup stock; cover pan and cook 20 minutes or until onion is soft. Return chicken and juice, if any, to pan. Add additional stock, if necessary, and green pepper and salt. Cook, covered, over medium heat 25 to 30 minutes or until chicken is tender. Skim fat from surface. Heat remaining 1 tablespoon shortening in small saucepan; blend in 2 tablespoons paprika. Stir until heated; *do not burn.* Blend into cooking liquid. Remove ½ cup cooking liquid from pan. Place in small bowl; whisk in sour cream and yogurt. Pour sour cream mixture over chicken; remove immediately from heat.

Turkey Italian

Makes 8 servings.

- 1 8-ounce package spaghetti, cooked and drained
- 2 cups sliced fresh mushrooms
- ¼ cup butter or margarine
- 2 tablespoons all-purpose flour
- 2 cups chicken broth or bouillon
- 1 8-ounce container plain yogurt
- 1 teaspoon granulated sugar
- 3 tablespoons sherry
- 1 teaspoon salt
  Dash pepper
- ⅛ teaspoon nutmeg
- 3 cups cubed cooked turkey
- ¼ cup grated Parmesan cheese

Preheat oven to 375°. Sauté mushrooms in 2 tablespoons butter in large skillet until tender. Combine mushrooms and spaghetti in large buttered casserole. Melt 2 tablespoons butter in saucepan; blend in flour. Add chicken broth; stir until thickened. Remove from heat; add yogurt, sugar, sherry, salt, pepper, nutmeg and turkey. Pour over spaghetti mixture. Sprinkle with Parmesan cheese. Bake 20 to 25 minutes until heated thoroughly and lightly browned.

Curried Chicken with Fruit

Makes 4 to 5 servings.

- 1 3-pound frying chicken, quartered
- 1 6-pound capacity Brown-in-the-Oven Bag
- 1 32-ounce container plain yogurt
- 1 tablespoon curry powder
  Pinch ginger
- ¼ cup apricot preserves
- 1 clove garlic, crushed
- 1 medium onion, chopped
- 1 cup long grain rice (not instant), uncooked
  Salt and pepper to taste
- ¼ cup golden raisins
- 1 scallion, finely chopped

Preheat oven to 350°. Place chicken in bag, skin side down; set aside. Blend yogurt, curry powder, ginger, apricot preserves, garlic, onion, rice, salt, pepper and raisins together. Pour into bag with chicken; close with bag tie. Turn bag until chicken is thoroughly coated with yogurt mixture. Place in baking pan, with chicken skin side up. Pierce the bag to let steam escape. Bake 1 hour. Place chicken and rice on serving platter; garnish with chopped scallion.

Almond-Chicken Casserole

Makes 6 servings.

- 1 8-ounce container plain yogurt
- ½ cup mayonnaise
- ¼ cup dry white wine
- ½ teaspoon salt
- ½ teaspoon dried parsley
- ½ teaspoon dried dillweed
  Dash pepper
- ¼ teaspoon garlic powder
- 1 8-ounce package wide noodles, cooked and drained
- 1 10-ounce package French-style frozen green beans, cooked and drained
- 2 cups cubed cooked chicken
- 1 cup slivered almonds
- ⅓ cup grated Parmesan cheese
  Paprika

Preheat oven to 350°. Combine first 8 ingredients. Layer ½ each of noodles, beans, chicken, almonds, cheese and sauce in a 3-quart casserole. Repeat layers. Sprinkle with paprika. Bake uncovered 30 minutes or until thoroughly heated.

Savory Chicken Stew

Makes 4 to 6 servings.

   3 tablespoons butter *or* margarine
1½ teaspoons salt
  ¾ teaspoon pepper
   1 frying chicken, cut in serving pieces
   1 tablespoon paprika
 12 small onions
  ½ pound mushrooms, sliced
   2 tablespoons chopped celery leaves
   1 cup sliced celery
1½ cups chicken broth
1½ cups dry white wine
  ½ teaspoon crushed thyme
   1 teaspoon cornstarch
  ½ cup plain yogurt

Melt 2 tablespoons butter in large skillet. Sprinkle 1 teaspoon salt and ¼ teaspoon pepper over chicken. Brown chicken in butter; remove. Stir paprika into butter in skillet; add remaining tablespoon butter. Add onions, mushrooms and celery leaves; cover and cook over low heat 5 minutes. Return chicken to skillet; add celery, broth, wine, thyme and remaining salt and pepper. Cover and simmer 25 minutes until chicken is tender. Mix cornstarch and yogurt in small bowl. Stir into chicken mixture. Heat thoroughly.

Cornish Hens in Mushroom Sauce

Makes 4 servings.

   2 1-pound Cornish hens, thawed and cut into
     halves lengthwise
     Salt and freshly ground black pepper to taste
   3 tablespoons butter
   1 medium onion, finely chopped
   1 cup thinly sliced mushrooms
  ½ cup dry white wine
   2 medium tomatoes, peeled, deseeded and diced
   1 large garlic clove, minced
   1 tablespoon chopped fresh basil *or*
   1 teaspoon crushed dried basil
   2 teaspoons finely chopped fresh marjoram *or*
  ½ teaspoon crushed dried marjoram
   1 teaspoon finely chopped fresh thyme *or*
  ¼ teaspoon crushed dried thyme
  ½ cup plain yogurt
   1 tablespoon flour

Preheat oven to 400°. Lightly sprinkle hens with salt and pepper. Arrange in baking pan. Roast, uncovered, 20 minutes. Melt butter in heavy skillet over moderate heat. Add onion and mushrooms; sauté until lightly browned, stirring frequently. Remove from heat and stir in wine, tomatoes, garlic, basil, marjoram, thyme and salt and pepper to taste. Spoon mixture over hens.

Reduce oven temperature to 350°. Cover baking pan; bake 25 minutes or until hens are tender. Remove hens to heated serving platter; keep warm. Transfer mushrooms and juices from baking dish to small saucepan. Blend yogurt and flour until smooth in small bowl; add to saucepan and simmer until thickened, stirring constantly. Taste and adjust seasoning. Pour into heated gravy boat; serve immediately.

Chicken Breasts de Valaille

Makes 4 servings.

   4 large chicken breasts, skinned and boned
     Salt and white pepper to taste
  ¼ cup lemon juice
  ¼ cup butter *or* margarine
   2 tablespoons finely chopped onion
1½ cups sliced fresh mushrooms
  ¼ cup chicken broth
  ¼ cup dry white wine
   2 teaspoons all-purpose flour
1½ cups plain yogurt
     Hot cooked rice

Sprinkle chicken breasts with salt and pepper and 1 tablespoon of lemon juice. Sauté chicken in butter in large skillet until golden brown and cooked thoroughly. Remove from heat; keep warm. Add onion and mushrooms to pan drippings; sauté until tender. Add chicken broth and wine; cook over high heat until slightly thickened. Stir in flour and yogurt; cook over low heat, stirring constantly until thickened. Adjust seasoning and add remaining lemon juice. Serve with rice.

Grilled Chicken

Makes 4 servings.

   1 8-ounce container plain yogurt
  ¼ cup wine vinegar
   1 tablespoon lemon juice
   1 garlic clove, minced
   1 teaspoon ground coriander
   1 teaspoon dry mustard
  ½ teaspoon freshly ground pepper
  ½ teaspoon ground ginger
  ⅛ teaspoon ground cloves
   5 drops Tabasco sauce
   1 2-pound frying chicken, cut up and fat trimmed

Combine all ingredients except chicken in large bowl; mix well. Add chicken, turning to coat; marinate in refrigerator 1½ hours. Remove chicken and place, skin-side up, on grill 7 inches from heat; reserve marinade. Cook, turning and basting with marinade, 1 hour or until done.

Vegetables

Crunchy Carrots

Makes 4 to 6 servings.

- 8 carrots, cooked and cut lengthwise
- 1 egg, beaten
- ½ cup dry bread crumbs
- ¼ cup olive oil
- ½ cup plain yogurt, room temperature
- ¼ teaspoon salt

Dip carrots in egg; roll in bread crumbs. Heat olive oil in skillet over medium heat. Fry carrots until golden. Place on serving platter. Combine yogurt and salt; drizzle over carrots. Serve immediately.

Summer Green Beans

Makes 4 servings.

- 1½ cups plain yogurt
- ⅓ cup chopped fresh parsley
- 3 tablespoons fresh lemon juice
- 3 tablespoons Dijon mustard
  Salt and freshly ground pepper to taste
- 1 pound fresh green beans, parboiled and cut in 2-inch pieces
  Butter lettuce
  Capers and chopped parsley for garnish

Combine yogurt, parsley, lemon juice, mustard, salt and pepper in large bowl. Stir in beans. Arrange lettuce on platter; spoon beans into center. Garnish with capers and parsley. Excellent with cold meats, poultry and fish.

Broccoli with Mornay Sauce

Makes 4 servings.

- ¼ cup bread crumbs
- ⅓ cup grated Parmesan cheese
- 1 tablespoon chopped fresh parsley
- 1 teaspoon paprika
- ¼ teaspoon garlic powder
- 4 cups cooked broccoli, cut into bite-size pieces
- 2 tablespoons butter or margarine
- 2 tablespoons flour
- 1 8-ounce container plain yogurt
- 3 ounces Swiss cheese, cut into small pieces

Preheat oven to 350°. Combine bread crumbs, 1½ tablespoons Parmesan cheese, parsley, paprika and garlic powder in a bowl. Place broccoli in a 1-quart baking dish. Melt butter in top of double boiler over boiling water. Stir in flour using a wire whisk. Add yogurt; continue to stir. Add Swiss cheese and remaining Parmesan. Stir until cheese melts. Pour sauce over broccoli. Sprin-

kle evenly with bread crumb mixture. Bake 30 minutes or until top is golden.

Broiled Tomatoes

Makes 8 servings.

- 4 medium tomatoes
- ½ cup plain yogurt
  Dash freshly ground pepper
  Dash garlic salt
- 2 tablespoons bread crumbs
- 1 tablespoon chopped parsley

Cut tomatoes in half crosswise. Mix yogurt, pepper and garlic salt. Spread over tomato halves. Sprinkle with bread crumbs. Broil about 6 inches from heat, until topping is golden and tomatoes are soft. Garnish with chopped parsley.

Corn Pudding

Makes 4 servings.

- 2 large eggs
- 1½ cups fresh cooked corn or 1 12-ounce can whole kernel corn, drained
- 3 tablespoons flour
- ¾ teaspoon salt
- ⅛ teaspoon white pepper
- 2 tablespoons melted butter or margarine
- 1 8-ounce container plain yogurt
- ⅔ cup milk

Preheat oven to 325°. Beat eggs in bowl; add remaining ingredients as listed. Pour mixture into buttered 1½-quart baking dish. Place dish in a pan of hot water 1 inch deep. Bake 1 hour or until knife inserted into center comes out clean.

Cauliflower Casserole

Makes 6 servings.

- 1 8-ounce container plain yogurt, room temperature
- 1 10¾-ounce can cream of shrimp soup
- ½ cup milk
- 1 tablespoon flour
- 2 tablespoons butter or margarine, melted
- 1 medium head cauliflower, cut into flowerets, cooked and drained
- ¼ cup chopped pecans

Preheat oven to 350°. Stir yogurt in a bowl until creamy; fold in soup. Stir in milk and flour. Drizzle butter into mixture, stirring constantly. Arrange cauliflowerets in buttered 2½-quart casserole. Pour mixture over cauliflower; sprinkle with pecans. Bake 25 minutes.

Vegetables

Mashed Sweet Potatoes

Makes 6 servings.

- 2 pounds sweet potatoes
- 2 tablespoons butter *or* margarine
- ¾ cup pineapple-orange yogurt
- 1 tablespoon granulated sugar
- ¾ teaspoon salt *or* to taste

Cook sweet potatoes in boiling salted water until tender, about 45 minutes. Peel potatoes; add butter and mash until smooth. Stir in yogurt, sugar and salt. Serve immediately.

Squash with Yogurt-Dill Sauce

Makes 6 servings.

- 3 tablespoons butter *or* margarine
- 1 pound zucchini, sliced ½-inch thick
- 1 pound yellow summer squash, sliced ½-inch thick
- ½ cup finely chopped onion
- 2 tablespoons chopped fresh dill *or* 2 teaspoons dried dillweed
- 1 tablespoon lemon juice
- ½ teaspoon salt
- ¼ teaspoon garlic powder
  Fresh dill to garnish

Melt butter in large skillet. Add zucchini, summer squash and onion; toss gently to mix. Cover and cook over low heat 5 to 8 minutes or until squash is tender. Combine remaining ingredients; add to mixture. Heat thoroughly. Garnish with dill.

Herb-Stuffed Baked Potatoes

Makes 6 servings.

- 6 medium baking potatoes
- ½ cup butter *or* margarine, softened
- 1 8-ounce container plain yogurt
- ¾ teaspoon rosemary
- ¾ teaspoon parsley flakes
- ⅛ teaspoon sage
- ¾ teaspoon salt
  Dash white pepper
- 1 tablespoon butter *or* margarine, melted
  Minced parsley for garnish

Preheat oven to 350°. Pierce potato skins with a fork. Bake 1 hour until tender. Cut slice from top. Scoop out pulp; set shells aside. Mash potatoes. Add butter; beat until creamy. Add yogurt, rosemary, parsley, sage, salt and white pepper; beat until fluffy. Fill potato shells. Brush lightly with melted butter. Place in shallow baking dish. Increase oven temperature to 400°. Bake 15 minutes until lightly browned. Garnish with parsley.

Eggplant with Yogurt

Makes 4 to 6 servings.

- 1 medium (about 1½ pounds) eggplant, cut in half
- ¼ cup vegetable oil
- 3 medium onions, chopped
- 2 cloves garlic, crushed
- 1 teaspoon ground ginger
- 1 teaspoon coriander
- 1 teaspoon cumin
- ¼ teaspoon cayenne pepper
- 1 teaspoon salt
- 1 8-ounce container plain yogurt
- ½ teaspoon granulated sugar

Bake eggplant, cut side down, in oiled shallow baking dish at 350° for 30 minutes or until tender. Cool; peel and cut into cubes. Heat 2 tablespoons oil in a large skillet. Sauté onion and garlic until golden. Stir in spices and salt; add remaining oil and eggplant. Cook 5 minutes. Just before serving, stir in yogurt and sugar.

Artichokes with Piquant Sauce

Makes 4 servings.

- 4 medium artichokes
  Lemon juice
- ½ cup plain yogurt
- ½ cup mayonnaise
- 2 to 3 tablespoons chopped pimiento
- 2 tablespoons finely chopped parsley
- 2 tablespoons finely chopped onion
- 2 tablespoons drained pickle relish

Wash and trim stems of artichokes. Cut 1 inch off of top. Remove loose outer leaves; trim sharp leaf tips. Brush cut edges with lemon juice. Cook artichokes in boiling water 20 to 30 minutes. Drain upside down; set aside. Blend all remaining ingredients in small bowl; chill 1 hour. Spoon sauce into artichokes before serving.

Zucchini Custard Casserole

Makes 6 servings.

- 4 slices bacon
- 2 cups thinly sliced zucchini
- 1 large onion, finely chopped
- 2 or 3 cloves garlic, minced *or* pressed
- 6 eggs
- ¾ teaspoon salt
- ½ teaspoon Italian herb seasoning *or* ¼ teaspoon each basil, oregano and rosemary
- 1 8-ounce container plain yogurt
- 2 cups cooked rice
- 1 cup shredded Cheddar cheese

Preheat oven to 350°. Fry bacon until crisp; drain and crumble. Reserve 2 tablespoons drippings. Sauté zucchini, onion and garlic in drippings, stirring, until tender; set aside. Beat eggs with salt, herb seasoning and yogurt in bowl until blended. Stir in rice, cheese, zucchini mixture and bacon. Pour into a buttered, shallow 2-quart casserole. Bake 35 minutes or until top is golden brown and center appears set. Let stand 5 minutes prior to serving.

Saucy Noodles

Makes 4 servings.

    3 tablespoons butter
    ½ cup finely chopped shallots or scallions
    2 tablespoons flour
    1 cup half-and-half
    1 8-ounce container plain yogurt
    ¼ teaspoon ground nutmeg
      Salt and white pepper to taste
    8 ounces spinach noodles or medium egg noodles,
      cooked and drained
      Freshly grated Parmesan cheese

Melt butter in saucepan over medium heat. Add shallots; sauté until soft and golden, stirring frequently. Add flour; cook, stirring, about 2 minutes. Gradually stir in half-and-half and yogurt. Cook over low heat until sauce is smooth, thickened and heated. Add nutmeg, salt and pepper; taste and adjust seasoning. Place noodles in heated serving dish; cover with sauce, tossing gently to coat. Sprinkle with Parmesan cheese. Serve immediately.

Turkish Carrots

Makes 6 servings.

    6 large carrots, scraped and cut into thin
      lengthwise strips
    2 teaspoons fresh lemon juice
    ½ cup flour
    ½ teaspoon salt
    ¼ cup chicken bouillon
    1½ cups olive oil
    1 egg white, stiffly beaten
    1 8-ounce container plain yogurt
    1 clove garlic, mashed

Sprinkle carrots with lemon juice; set aside. Combine flour, salt, bouillon and 1 tablespoon oil; mix until smooth. Fold in egg white. Heat remaining oil in skillet until hot. Dip carrot slices into batter; fry until brown and crisp. Drain on paper toweling. Blend yogurt and garlic together; pour over carrots. Serve immediately.

Blue Cheese-Stuffed Potatoes

Makes 8 servings.

    4 large baking potatoes
    ¼ cup butter or margarine, softened
    1 8-ounce container plain yogurt
    ½ cup milk
    8 slices bacon, cooked, drained and crumbled
    ¼ cup chopped scallions
    2 to 3 tablespoons crumbled blue cheese
    1 teaspoon Dijon mustard
    1½ teaspoons salt
    ¼ teaspoon pepper
      Paprika

Preheat oven to 400°. Rub potato skins with butter and pierce with fork. Bake 1 hour or until tender. Cut each potato in half lengthwise and scoop out pulp, leaving ⅛-inch thick shell. Mash potatoes until smooth. Beat in yogurt and milk; blend well. Stir in remaining ingredients except paprika. Refill shells with potato mixture. Sprinkle with paprika. Arrange in baking dish and refrigerate until ready to serve; reheat at 400° 15 to 20 minutes until piping hot.

Spinach Pudding

Makes 4 servings.

    2 tablespoons butter
    1 tablespoon minced shallots or scallions
    2 tablespoons flour
    ¾ cup plain yogurt
      Salt and pepper to taste
    ⅛ to ¼ teaspoon nutmeg
      Pinch of cayenne pepper, optional
    2 pounds fresh spinach, chopped and
      cooked or 2 10-ounce packages frozen
      chopped spinach, cooked
    2 eggs, lightly beaten

Preheat oven to 375°. Melt butter in saucepan; add shallots and cook over medium heat until soft. Add flour; stir until blended. Cook 1 to 2 minutes. Add yogurt; cook, stirring, until thick and bubbly. Season with salt, pepper, nutmeg and cayenne pepper. Mix in spinach; remove from heat. Cool. Add eggs, stirring well. Butter a 4-cup baking dish; pour in mixture. Set baking dish in pan containing about ½-inch hot water; place on rack in lower third of oven. Bake 35 minutes or until puffed and golden brown.

Breads & Muffins

Yogurt White Bread

Makes 2 loaves.

5¾ to 6¼ cups flour
2 packages active dry yeast
1 cup milk
2 tablespoons granulated sugar
2 tablespoons butter
1¾ teaspoons salt
1½ cups plain yogurt
Softened butter

Combine 2 cups flour and yeast in large bowl. Heat milk, sugar, butter and salt in saucepan until warm (115 to 120°). Add to dry ingredients. Add yogurt; blend well. Stir in enough additional flour to make a soft dough. Knead 10 minutes, until dough is smooth and elastic. Place in buttered bowl; brush dough with softened butter. Cover and let rise until double in bulk, about 1 hour. Punch dough down; divide in half. Shape each into smooth ball; let rest 10 minutes. Shape into 2 loaves; put in 2 greased 9 x 5 x 3-inch loaf pans. Cover and let rise until double in bulk, 45 to 60 minutes. Preheat oven to 425°. Bake 25 to 30 minutes, until browned and loaf sounds hollow when tapped. If tops brown too quickly, cover loosely with foil last 10 minutes. Remove from pans; cool on wire racks.

Rye Yogurt Bread

Makes 2 loaves.

2 packages active dry yeast
1 teaspoon granulated sugar
½ cup warm water (110 to 115°)
2 8-ounce containers plain yogurt, room temperature
2 tablespoons peanut oil
1 tablespoon salt
½ cup wheat flour
2 cups rye flour
4 cups flour
Softened butter
Cornmeal

Dissolve yeast and sugar in water. Let stand 5 minutes. Combine yogurt and peanut oil in large bowl. Add yeast mixture and salt. Stir in wheat and rye flours until well-blended. Add flour, 1 cup at a time, to make a soft dough. Knead dough on lightly floured surface 10 minutes or until firm and elastic. Shape dough into ball and place in well-buttered bowl, turning to coat with but-

ter. Cover with towel and place in warm, draft-free place until double in bulk, about 45 minutes. Punch down and allow to rise again until double in bulk, about 30 minutes. After second rising, punch down, turn out on lightly floured board and divide into two equal parts. Shape into 2 loaves, either free-form or to fit into well-buttered 8 x 4 x 2-inch loaf pans. Place free-form loaves on buttered baking sheet sprinkled with cornmeal and let rise until almost doubled in size, or let loaves rise, covered, in pans. Brush loaves with cold water. Preheat oven to 400°. Bake 15 minutes; reduce heat to 375° and bake 45 minutes or until loaves sound hollow when tapped. Cool thoroughly on wire racks.

Whole Wheat Muffins

Makes 1 dozen.

1 cup whole wheat flour
1 cup flour
1 tablespoon baking powder
½ teaspoon salt
2 eggs, lightly beaten
⅓ cup honey
¼ cup vegetable oil
1 8-ounce container apple yogurt

Preheat oven to 400°. Combine flour, baking powder and salt in large bowl. Blend eggs, honey and oil together in small bowl; stir in yogurt. Stir yogurt mixture into flour mixture just until dry ingredients are moistened. Spoon into greased muffin cups. Bake 18 to 20 minutes.

Yogurt Bran Muffins

Makes 1 dozen.

1¾ cups flour
1 cup bran cereal
1 tablespoon baking powder
½ teaspoon baking soda
½ teaspoon salt
1 egg, beaten
1 8-ounce container plain yogurt
3 tablespoons vegetable oil
3 tablespoons honey
2 tablespoons milk

Preheat oven to 400°. Stir dry ingredients together in large bowl. Blend remaining ingredients together in separate bowl. Add liquid to flour mixture, stirring only until flour is moistened. Spoon into greased muffin cups. Bake 20 to 25 minutes or until golden brown.

Banana Date-Nut Muffins, page 44

Breads & Muffins

Pear Yogurt Muffins

Makes approximately 1 dozen.

    2 cups sifted flour
    ½ cup granulated sugar
    1½ teaspoons baking powder
    1 teaspoon baking soda
    ½ teaspoon salt
    1 8-ounce container plain yogurt, room temperature
    1 egg, lightly beaten
    ¼ cup vegetable oil or melted shortening
    2 teaspoons grated lemon peel
    1 16-ounce can pears, drained and diced

Preheat oven to 400°. Sift dry ingredients together in large bowl; set aside. Stir yogurt until creamy in small bowl; blend in egg. Drizzle oil into yogurt-egg mixture; blend well. Add lemon peel. Pour into flour mixture. Gently fold in pears. Stir just until flour mixture is moistened. Fill greased muffin cups ⅔ full. Bake 20 to 25 minutes until golden brown. Remove from pan immediately. Serve warm.

Cornmeal Muffins

Makes 1 dozen.

    1 cup flour
    ¾ cup yellow cornmeal
    ⅓ cup granulated sugar
    ¼ teaspoon salt
    ½ teaspoon baking soda
    ⅓ cup shortening
    1 egg, lightly beaten
    1 8-ounce container plain yogurt
    ¼ cup butter, melted

Preheat oven to 375°. Sift dry ingredients in large bowl. Cut in shortening until mixture resembles coarse meal. Combine egg, yogurt and butter in small bowl; add to dry mixture, stirring just until moistened. Spoon batter into greased muffin cups or mini-muffin pans. Bake 18 to 20 minutes or until golden.

Blueberry Muffins

Makes 1 dozen.

    2 cups flour
    1 teaspoon baking powder
    ½ teaspoon salt
    2 tablespoons butter or margarine
    ¾ cup plain or blueberry yogurt
    2 tablespoons honey
    ½ cup fresh blueberries

Preheat oven to 375°. Sift flour, baking powder and salt together in large bowl; blend in butter with fork. Blend in yogurt and honey; add blueberries, stirring only enough to distribute them evenly. Fill paper-lined or lightly greased muffin cups ⅔ full; bake 20 minutes.

Note: Toss berries with flour before mixing into batter to prevent streaking.

Banana Date-Nut Muffins

Makes 15.

    3 medium bananas, mashed
    2 eggs, lightly beaten
    ¼ cup plain yogurt
    ¼ cup vegetable oil
    1 cup flour
    1 cup whole wheat flour
    ⅓ cup granulated sugar
    2 teaspoons baking powder
    ¼ teaspoon cinnamon
    ¼ teaspoon salt
    ¾ cup chopped dates
    ½ cup chopped walnuts

Preheat oven to 400°. Combine bananas, eggs, yogurt and oil in large bowl. Stir dry ingredients together in separate large bowl. Add banana mixture to flour mixture, stirring only until moistened. Stir in dates and walnuts. Spoon into well-greased muffin tins. Bake 20 to 25 minutes or until lightly browned.

Apple Yogurt Muffins

Makes 1 dozen.

    1½ cups biscuit mix
    ¼ cup granulated sugar
    ½ teaspoon cinnamon
    ¼ teaspoon ground cloves
    ⅛ teaspoon allspice
    ¼ cup cold butter
    1 egg, lightly beaten
    ½ cup apple yogurt
      Streusel Topping

Preheat oven to 400°. Combine biscuit mix, sugar and spices in bowl. Cut in butter with pastry blender until crumbly. Stir in egg and yogurt, mixing only until moistened. Spoon batter into 12 greased or paper-lined muffin cups. Sprinkle with Streusel Topping. Bake 20 minutes or until pick inserted in center comes out clean.

Streusel Topping

    1 tablespoon butter, softened
    2 tablespoons granulated sugar
    ¼ cup flour
    ¼ cup finely chopped walnuts

Combine butter, sugar and flour until crumbly in small bowl. Stir in walnuts.

Lemon Tea Bread

Makes 1 loaf.

- ¾ cup granulated sugar
- 2 tablespoons butter *or* margarine, melted
- ¼ cup fresh lemon juice
- 1 egg
- 2 cups flour
- 2 teaspoons baking powder
- ½ teaspoon salt
- 1 8-ounce container lemon yogurt
- 1 tablespoon grated lemon rind
- ½ cup chopped pecans

Preheat oven to 350°. Combine sugar, butter and lemon juice in bowl. Add egg; beat until smooth. Sift flour, baking powder and salt in separate bowl. Stir into creamed mixture alternately with yogurt just until blended. Add rind and pecans. Spoon batter into greased 8 x 4-inch loaf pan. Bake 1 hour or until wooden pick inserted in center comes out clean.

Oatmeal Raisin Bread

Makes 1 loaf.

- 1 cup flour
- 1 cup medium rye flour
- 1 teaspoon baking soda
- 1 teaspoon baking powder
- 1 teaspoon salt
- 2 tablespoons granulated sugar
- 1 cup rolled oats
- ¼ cup light molasses
- 1¼ cups plain yogurt
- 1 cup raisins

Preheat oven to 350°. Stir flours, baking soda, baking powder, salt and sugar together in large bowl. Mix in rolled oats. Combine yogurt and molasses; add to dry mixture. Stir in raisins. Pour into greased 8 x 4-inch loaf pan. Bake 1 hour or until wooden pick inserted in center comes out clean. After cooking, wrap in foil and let stand 1 day before serving.

Quick Cranberry Muffins

Makes 1 dozen.

- ¾ cup chopped fresh cranberries
- ½ cup granulated sugar
- 2 cups biscuit mix
- 1 egg
- 1 8-ounce container plain yogurt

Preheat oven to 400°. Combine cranberries and ¼ cup sugar; let stand 15 minutes. Combine remaining sugar and biscuit mix in bowl; blend well. Beat egg in small bowl; add yogurt. Add to biscuit mixture; stir until dry ingredients are moistened. Fold in cranberries. Fill well-greased muffin cups ¾ full. Bake 25 minutes.

Cinnamon Yogurt Muffins

Makes 1 dozen.

- ¾ cup margarine, softened
- 1¼ cups granulated sugar
- 2 eggs
- 1 teaspoon vanilla
- 1 8-ounce container plain yogurt
- 2 cups flour
- 1 teaspoon baking powder
- ½ teaspoon baking soda
- 1 teaspoon salt
- 2 tablespoons granulated sugar
- 1 teaspoon cinnamon

Preheat oven to 400°. Cream margarine, 1¼ cups sugar, eggs and vanilla in large bowl. Add yogurt; blend well. Combine flour, baking powder, baking soda and salt in separate bowl. Add to sugar mixture, blending only until all ingredients are moistened. Fill greased muffin cups ½ full. Combine 2 tablespoons sugar and cinnamon; sprinkle one-half of the mixture over batter in each cup. Fill each cup with remaining batter and sprinkle with remaining cinnamon-sugar mixture. Bake 15 to 20 minutes.

Yogurt Scones

Makes 2 dozen.

- ½ cup currants *or* seedless raisins
- 2½ to 2¾ cups flour
- ½ teaspoon salt
- ½ cup granulated sugar
- 2 teaspoons baking powder
- 1 teaspoon baking soda
- 6 tablespoons cold butter
- 1 egg, lightly beaten
- 1 8-ounce container plain yogurt
- Grated rind of ½ lemon

Preheat oven to 425°. Toss currants in 2 tablespoons flour; set aside. Sift remaining flour with salt, sugar, baking powder and baking soda into large bowl. Cut in butter with pastry blender until crumbly. Add currants, egg, yogurt and lemon rind to flour mixture; blend well. Divide dough into 24 balls. Flatten to ½ inch thick. Arrange on lightly greased cookie sheet. Bake 12 minutes or until lightly browned. Cool on wire racks or serve warm with butter and jam.

Three Cheers Brownies

Makes 16.

½ cup butter *or* margarine, softened
1 cup granulated sugar
2 eggs
1 teaspoon vanilla
1 cup flour
½ teaspoon baking powder
½ teaspoon salt
¼ teaspoon baking soda
1 8-ounce container plain yogurt
2 1-ounce squares unsweetened chocolate, melted and cooled
Confectioners' sugar

Preheat oven to 350°. Prepare Crust; set aside. Cream butter and sugar until light and fluffy in large bowl. Add eggs and vanilla; mix well. Combine dry ingredients in separate bowl; stir into creamed mixture. Add yogurt and melted chocolate; mix well. Pour batter over prepared Crust. Bake 45 minutes or until wooden pick inserted in the center of dough comes out clean. Cool completely on wire rack. Dust with confectioners' sugar; cut into squares.

Crust

1 cup quick cooking *or* old-fashioned rolled oats
½ cup flour
½ cup firmly packed brown sugar
¼ teaspoon salt
6 tablespoons butter, melted

Combine oats, flour, brown sugar and salt in bowl. Stir in melted butter until well blended. Press onto the bottom of 9-inch square baking pan. Bake 10 minutes. Remove from oven.

Old-Fashioned Scotch Oatmeal Cookies

Makes 4½ dozen.

¾ cup butter *or* margarine, softened
1 cup dark brown sugar
½ cup granulated sugar
1 egg
½ cup plain yogurt
1 teaspoon Drambuie
1 cup flour
1 teaspoon salt
½ teaspoon baking soda
3 cups rolled oats

Preheat oven to 350°. Cream butter in bowl; add sugars and blend well. Add egg, yogurt and Drambuie, beating after each addition. Combine flour, salt and baking soda; stir into creamed mixture. Add oats; mix well. Drop by teaspoonfuls onto greased cookie sheets. Bake 12 minutes.

Yogurt Raisin Cookies

Makes 4 dozen.

½ cup butter, softened
1 cup packed brown sugar
1 egg
2 cups sifted flour
2 teaspoons baking powder
½ teaspoon salt
½ teaspoon baking soda
½ teaspoon nutmeg
½ cup plain yogurt
½ cup seedless raisins
¾ cup chopped nuts

Preheat oven to 400°. Cream butter and sugar until light and fluffy. Beat in egg. Sift dry ingredients together; add to creamed mixture alternately with yogurt. Beat until smooth; stir in raisins and nuts. Drop by teaspoonfuls onto lightly greased cookie sheets. Bake 10 to 12 minutes.

Chocolate Chip Cream Cookies

Makes 7 to 8 dozen.

½ cup butter *or* margarine, softened
1½ cups firmly packed light brown sugar
2 eggs
1 teaspoon vanilla
2½ cups flour
1 teaspoon baking soda
½ teaspoon baking powder
½ teaspoon salt
1 8-ounce container plain yogurt
1 12-ounce package semisweet chocolate chips
1 cup chopped nuts

Preheat oven to 375°. Cream butter in bowl; gradually add sugar. Beat until light and fluffy; add eggs and vanilla. Sift flour, baking soda, baking powder and salt together; add to creamed mixture alternately with yogurt, beginning and ending with dry ingredients. Stir in chocolate chips and nuts. Drop by rounded teaspoonfuls onto greased baking sheets. Bake 10 to 12 minutes. Remove immediately to wire rack to cool.

Cookies

Orange Bars

Makes 4 dozen.

1½ cups flour
½ teaspoon baking soda
¼ teaspoon salt
½ cup butter *or* margarine, softened
1 cup granulated sugar
1 large egg
1 tablespoon grated orange rind
1 teaspoon vanilla
⅓ cup plain yogurt
⅓ cup orange marmalade
½ cup finely chopped walnuts
3 tablespoons granulated sugar
3 tablespoons orange juice

Preheat oven to 350°. Sift flour, baking soda and salt together; set aside. Cream butter and 1 cup sugar in large bowl; beat in egg, orange rind and vanilla. Stir in flour mixture alternately with yogurt; blend in marmalade. Spread evenly in well-greased 15 x 10 x 1-inch jelly-roll pan; sprinkle with walnuts. Bake 25 minutes. Combine 3 tablespoons sugar and orange juice in small bowl for topping. Remove pan from oven and spoon topping over hot cake. Cut into 2 x 1½-inch bars while warm.

Carrot Yogurt Squares

Makes 24.

2 cups whole wheat flour
1 cup flour
2 teaspoons baking soda
1 teaspoon baking powder
1 teaspoon salt
1 teaspoon grated lemon peel
1 8-ounce container lemon *or* orange yogurt
1 cup finely grated carrot
¾ cup honey
½ cup chopped nuts
½ cup raisins, optional
2 eggs
⅓ cup vegetable oil
¼ cup milk

Preheat oven to 350°. Sift flour, soda, baking powder and salt together in large bowl. Blend remaining ingredients together in separate bowl. Add liquid mixture to flour mixture, stirring only until flour is moistened. Spread batter in greased 9 x 13-inch baking pan. Bake 30 to 35 minutes. Cool and cut into squares.

Chewy Oatmeal Cookies

Makes 4 dozen.

½ cup flour
¼ cup granulated sugar
½ teaspoon baking powder
½ teaspoon baking soda
¼ teaspoon salt
¼ cup brown sugar
¼ cup butter *or* margarine, softened
1 egg
2 tablespoons plain yogurt
¼ teaspoon vanilla
1 cup quick-cooking rolled oats

Preheat oven to 375°. Combine flour, granulated sugar, baking powder, baking soda and salt in large bowl. Add brown sugar, butter, egg, yogurt and vanilla; beat well. Stir in rolled oats. Chill dough. Drop by teaspoonfuls onto ungreased baking sheets. Bake 8 minutes. Cool slightly before removing from baking sheet; cool on rack.

Molasses Sour Cream Cookies

Makes 4 dozen.

½ cup shortening
½ cup brown sugar
½ cup light molasses
1 egg
2 cups sifted flour
⅛ teaspoon allspice
½ teaspoon ground cloves
1 teaspoon cinnamon
½ teaspoon salt
1 teaspoon baking soda
½ cup plain yogurt
½ cup seedless raisins
1 cup coarsely chopped walnuts

Preheat oven to 375°. Cream shortening until light and fluffy. Add brown sugar; beat well. Stir in molasses. Add egg; mix well. Sift dry ingredients together; add to creamed mixture. Stir in yogurt, raisins and nuts. Drop by teaspoonfuls onto greased baking sheets. Bake 10 minutes.

Spice Cake

Makes 1 9 x 13-inch cake.

½ cup butter, softened
1½ cups granulated sugar
3 eggs, beaten
2 cups all-purpose flour
1 teaspoon baking powder
1 teaspoon baking soda
¼ teaspoon salt
1 teaspoon nutmeg
½ teaspoon cinnamon
1 8-ounce container plain yogurt
½ teaspoon vanilla

Preheat oven to 325°. Cream butter and sugar in large bowl until smooth; beat in eggs. Sift dry ingredients together in small bowl. Add flour mixture alternately with yogurt to creamed mixture. Add vanilla; blend well. Pour into a greased and floured 9 x 13-inch baking pan. Bake 45 minutes or until a toothpick inserted in center comes out clean. Remove from oven; cool. Prepare Topping; spread evenly over cake. Place under broiler until lightly browned.

Topping

1 tablespoon butter, softened
½ cup brown sugar
½ cup finely chopped walnuts
¾ cup shredded coconut
¼ cup heavy cream
¼ teaspoon vanilla
⅛ teaspoon ground nutmeg

Cream butter and brown sugar together. Add remaining ingredients; blend well.

Carrot Yogurt Cake

Makes 1 10-inch tube cake.

1 cup butter *or* margarine
1⅔ cups granulated sugar
4 eggs
1 teaspoon grated lemon peel
1 teaspoon cinnamon
1 teaspoon vanilla
1 8-ounce container plain yogurt
2½ cups all-purpose flour
1 teaspoon baking soda
1½ teaspoons baking powder
½ teaspoon salt
¾ cup chopped walnuts
2½ cups grated carrots

Preheat oven to 350°. Beat butter in large bowl until creamy; beat in sugar and eggs. Blend lemon peel, cinnamon, vanilla and yogurt into creamed mixture. Combine flour, baking soda, baking powder and salt in small bowl. Add flour mixture to creamed mixture; beat until smooth. Stir in nuts and carrots. Pour into a greased and floured 10-inch tube pan. Bake 70 minutes or until golden. Cool thoroughly; remove from pan.

Devil's Food Cake

Makes 1 9-inch cake.

2 cups sifted cake flour
1¼ teaspoons baking soda
½ teaspoon salt
½ cup butter *or* margarine, softened
1¼ cups granulated sugar
2 eggs
2 1-ounce squares unsweetened chocolate, melted and cooled
1 teaspoon vanilla extract
¾ cup plain yogurt, room temperature
⅓ cup boiling water
Fluffy Chocolate Icing

Preheat oven to 375°. Grease and lightly flour two 9-inch round cake pans; set aside. Sift cake flour, baking soda and salt together. Cream butter in large bowl; add sugar and beat until light and fluffy. Add eggs 1 at a time, beating well after each addition. Stir in melted chocolate and vanilla extract. Stir yogurt until creamy. Add flour mixture alternately with yogurt to creamed mixture, beginning and ending with flour mixture. Add boiling water; blend well. Pour into pans. Bake 25 to 30 minutes. Cool. Frost with Fluffy Chocolate Icing.

Fluffy Chocolate Icing

5 tablespoons butter, softened
2 1-ounce squares unsweetened chocolate, melted and cooled
3 cups sifted confectioners' sugar
¼ cup plain yogurt, room temperature
1 egg yolk
1 teaspoon vanilla extract

Combine all ingredients; beat until smooth.

Cakes

Lemon Yogurt Sponge Torte

Makes 8 to 10 servings.

    4 eggs, separated
    ¾ cup granulated sugar
    1½ tablespoons lemon juice
    1 teaspoon baking powder
    ½ teaspoon grated lemon peel
    1 cup shredded coconut, toasted
    ½ cup all-purpose flour
    2 8-ounce containers lemon yogurt
    ¾ cup heavy cream, whipped and sweetened to taste
      Lemon slices for garnish

Preheat oven to 375°. Lightly grease a 10 x 15-inch jelly-roll pan; line pan with waxed paper and lightly grease. Beat egg yolks, ½ cup sugar, lemon juice and baking powder in small bowl until thick and lemon-colored. Blend in lemon peel and ½ cup coconut. Beat egg whites in large bowl until soft peaks form. Gradually beat in remaining ¼ cup sugar until stiff peaks form. Gently fold egg yolk mixture and flour into beaten whites until blended; pour into prepared pan, spreading evenly. Bake 10 to 12 minutes or until top springs back when lightly touched. Cover a large wire rack (or two smaller racks) with waxed paper. Invert cake on rack and peel off paper; cool. Cut cake in half lengthwise. Place one half on serving platter and spread with yogurt. Place remaining layer on yogurt and spread with whipped cream. Garnish with remaining coconut and lemon slices. Chill 2 hours or overnight.

Orange Yogurt Cake

Makes 1 Bundt cake.

    1 cup butter or margarine, softened
    3 cups granulated sugar
    5 eggs
    1 teaspoon vanilla
    ¼ cup orange juice
    1½ tablespoons grated orange rind
    1 8-ounce container plain yogurt
    ½ teaspoon baking soda
    2¾ cups all-purpose flour
      Orange Glaze

Preheat oven to 350°. Generously grease 10-cup Bundt pan; set aside. Cream butter and sugar in large bowl until light and fluffy. Beat in eggs, 1 at a time, beating well after each addition. Add vanilla, orange juice and orange rind. Blend yogurt and baking soda in small bowl; add to creamed mixture alternately with flour. Pour into pan. Bake 45 to 50 minutes or until cake tester inserted in cake comes out clean. Cool in pan on wire rack about 40 minutes. Remove from pan; cool completely. Drizzle with glaze. Store in refrigerator.

Orange Glaze

    1 tablespoon butter or margarine, softened
    1 egg yolk
    2 cups confectioners' sugar
    1 teaspoon grated orange rind
    ½ cup orange juice

Combine all ingredients in small bowl; beat until smooth.

Apple Coffeecake

Makes 12 servings.

    2 cups unbleached flour
    3 teaspoons baking powder
    ¼ cup corn oil
    ¼ cup honey
    1 egg yolk
    1 8-ounce container plain yogurt, room temperature
    1 teaspoon vanilla extract
    3 egg whites, stiffly beaten
      Apple Topping
    2 tablespoons seedless raisins
    2 tablespoons chopped walnuts
    ½ teaspoon cinnamon

Preheat oven to 350°. Sift flour and baking powder into bowl. Combine oil, honey and egg yolk; beat lightly with fork. Add to dry ingredients alternately with yogurt and vanilla. Fold in stiffly beaten egg whites. Pour into lightly greased 9 x 13-inch baking pan, spreading evenly. Arrange Apple Topping on batter, pouring juices over cake. Sprinkle with raisins, walnuts and cinnamon, pressing mixture slightly into batter with spatula. Bake 50 minutes or until cake comes away slightly from sides of pan and is lightly browned (cake will be puddinglike). Cool in pan on wire rack. Cut into 12 pieces; remove carefully with spatula and serve slightly warm.

Apple Topping

    4 crisp apples, peeled, cored and sliced ¼ inch thick
      Juice of 1 small lemon
      Grated rind of ½ small lemon
    1 teaspoon corn oil
    2 tablespoons honey
    ½ teaspoon cinnamon
    ⅛ teaspoon ground cloves

Place apple slices in bowl with lemon juice and rind, turning to coat. Combine oil and honey in small bowl; add apple slices, tossing gently. Add cinnamon and cloves; mix and set aside.

Cakes

Baba Rhum Cake

Makes 1 Bundt cake.

- ½ cup butter *or* margarine, softened
- 2 cups granulated sugar
- 2 eggs
- 2½ cups all-purpose flour
- 1 teaspoon baking powder
  Pinch salt
- 1 8-ounce container plain yogurt
- ½ cup finely chopped almonds *or* walnuts
- 1 cup chopped candied fruit
- 2 tablespoons grated orange rind *or* 1 teaspoon orange extract
  Syrup

Cream butter and sugar in large bowl; beat in eggs. Blend in flour, baking powder and salt. Add yogurt, nuts, fruit and orange rind; blend well. Bake in an ungreased Bundt pan 40 minutes or until cake tester inserted in center comes out clean. Cool on wire rack 10 minutes; turn out on rack and cool completely. Serve with Syrup.

Syrup

- 1 small can orange juice concentrate
- 1 cup honey
- 2 tablespoons lemon juice
- ½ cup dark rum

Heat all ingredients in saucepan; stir until blended. Drizzle hot syrup over cake when served.

Banana Cake

Makes 1 10-inch tube cake.

- 1 cup butter *or* margarine, softened
- 1½ cups granulated sugar
- 4 eggs
- 1 teaspoon vanilla
- 3 cups sifted all-purpose flour
- 1 teaspoon baking soda
- ½ cup plain yogurt
- 1 cup mashed banana
  Banana slices for garnish, optional

Preheat oven to 350°. Cream butter and sugar in large bowl until light and fluffy. Add eggs, 1 at a time, beating well after each addition. Beat in vanilla. Sift flour and baking soda together in small bowl. Combine yogurt with mashed banana in separate small bowl. Beat flour mixture alternately with yogurt-banana mixture into creamed mixture. Pour into well-greased 10-inch tube pan. Bake 45 to 55 minutes or until cake tester inserted in center comes out clean. Cool in pan 10 to 20 minutes; remove to wire rack and cool completely. Garnish with banana slices, if desired.

Lemon Pound Cake

Makes 1 10-inch tube cake.

- 2¾ cups all-purpose flour
- 1 teaspoon baking soda
- ¼ teaspoon salt
- 6 eggs, separated
- ¼ teaspoon cream of tartar
- 2 cups granulated sugar
- 1 cup butter *or* margarine
- 1 tablespoon grated lemon peel
- 2 tablespoons lemon juice
- 1 8-ounce container lemon yogurt
  Confectioners' sugar, optional

Preheat oven to 350°. Combine flour, baking soda and salt in large bowl; set aside. Beat egg whites with cream of tartar in a separate bowl until soft peaks form. Gradually add ½ cup sugar, beating constantly until stiff; set aside. Cream butter in separate bowl; gradually add remaining 1½ cups sugar, beating until fluffy. Beat in egg yolks, lemon peel and lemon juice. Stir flour mixture alternately with yogurt into creamed mixture. Gently but thoroughly fold in egg whites. Pour into greased 10-inch tube pan. Bake 55 to 60 minutes. Cool in pan 10 minutes. Turn out on wire rack; cool completely. Sift confectioners' sugar over top, if desired.

Orange Date Coffeecake

Makes 1 9-inch square cake.

- ½ cup butter, softened
- 1 cup granulated sugar
- 2 eggs
- 1 8-ounce container plain yogurt
- 2½ cups all-purpose flour
- 1 teaspoon baking soda
- ¼ teaspoon salt
- 2 teaspoons grated orange peel
- ½ cup diced *or* chopped dates
- ½ cup orange juice
- ¼ cup rum

Preheat oven to 350°. Cream butter and ⅔ cup sugar in large bowl. Beat in eggs, 1 at a time. Blend in yogurt. Combine flour, baking soda, salt and orange peel in small bowl. Stir into egg mixture; add dates. Pour into greased and floured 9-inch square baking pan. Bake 50 to 55 minutes or until toothpick inserted into center comes out clean. Cool 15 minutes in pan. Invert onto wire rack. Heat remaining ⅓ cup sugar with orange juice and rum; stir to dissolve sugar. Pierce cake with fork at ½-inch intervals. Slowly pour glaze onto warm cake. Cover with plastic wrap. Cool. For best flavor, prepare 24 hours before serving.

Yogurt-Apple Pie

Makes 1 9-inch pie.

½ cup granulated sugar
2½ tablespoons flour
½ teaspoon cinnamon
  Dash nutmeg
4 cups peeled and sliced baking apples
1 egg, beaten
1 8-ounce container plain yogurt
½ teaspoon vanilla
½ teaspoon almond extract
1 unbaked 9-inch pastry shell

Preheat oven to 375°. Combine sugar, flour, cinnamon and nutmeg with apples in large bowl; set aside. Blend egg, yogurt, vanilla and almond extract in small bowl. Combine yogurt mixture with apple mixture. Pour into pie shell. Spoon Topping over pie; bake 45 to 50 minutes.

Topping

¼ cup cold butter *or* margarine
¼ cup brown sugar
¼ cup flour
2 tablespoons coconut
½ cup chopped walnuts

Combine butter, sugar and flour in bowl; blend with pastry blender until mixture crumbles to the size of peas. Stir in coconut and walnuts.

Fresh Peach Yogurt Pie

Makes 1 8-inch pie.

2 envelopes unflavored gelatin
½ cup water
1 10-ounce package frozen sliced peaches, slightly thawed, reserve liquid
2 8-ounce containers peach yogurt
1 8-inch graham cracker crust
3 large fresh peaches
1 tablespoon lemon juice
¼ cup apricot preserves

Sprinkle gelatin over water in top of double boiler; let stand 5 minutes to soften. Place softened gelatin over boiling water in double boiler; stir to dissolve gelatin. Remove from heat. Place peaches and liquid into blender or food processor; add gelatin. Blend until peaches are finely chopped and mixture thickens. Pour into bowl. Fold in yogurt thoroughly. Pour into graham cracker crust. Refrigerate about 8 hours until well chilled and firm enough to cut. To serve, peel peaches; slice and dip in lemon juice. Arrange slices over top of pie. Melt preserves over low heat and brush over peach slices.

Kiwi-Lime Pie

Makes 1 9-inch pie.

¾ cup granulated sugar
⅓ cup flour
⅛ teaspoon salt
1¾ cups milk
3 eggs, beaten
¼ cup butter *or* margarine, softened
2 teaspoons shredded lime rind
¼ cup fresh lime juice
1 8-ounce container lemon yogurt
  Green food coloring
  Pastry for 2-crust 9-inch pie
¼ cup apple jelly
½ pint heavy cream
1 tablespoon confectioners' sugar
2 to 3 kiwis, peeled and sliced
1 to 2 limes, sliced

Combine sugar, flour and salt in saucepan; stir in milk. Cook until thickened and bubbly, stirring constantly. Reduce heat; cook and stir 2 minutes. Remove from heat. Stir 1 cup of the hot mixture into eggs. Return to saucepan; cook and stir until thickened. Cook 2 additional minutes, stirring constantly; *do not boil.* Remove from heat. Stir in butter, lime rind and juice. Fold in yogurt; tint with food coloring. Cover with plastic wrap; cool. Preheat oven to 450°. Divide pastry in half. On floured surface roll one half to a ⅛-inch thickness. Line a 9-inch pie plate with pastry. Trim ½ inch beyond edge. Flute edge; prick pastry with fork. Bake 10 to 12 minutes. Cool. Divide remaining pastry in half. Roll each half to a ⅛-inch thickness. Cut an 8¾-inch circle from one portion and an 8-inch circle from other portion. Place circles on baking sheet; prick with fork. Bake 10 minutes; cool.

To assemble pie: Brush pastry shell with apple jelly. Place 1 cup lime filling in shell. Cover with 8-inch pastry. Brush with more jelly. Spread with 1¼ cups lime filling. Top with 8¾-inch pastry. Brush with remaining jelly. Top with remaining filling. Cover; chill overnight. To garnish, whip cream with confectioners' sugar and pipe in circle on top of pie. Arrange slices of kiwi and lime in circle.

Pies

Frozen Eggnog Pie

Makes 1 9-inch pie.

- 1 pint rum raisin ice cream, softened
- 1 pint honey ice cream, softened
- 1 8-ounce container frozen vanilla yogurt, softened
- 6 tablespoons bourbon
- ¾ teaspoon freshly ground nutmeg
- 1 baked 9-inch meringue shell
- 1 cup heavy cream
- 2 tablespoons confectioners' sugar
  Fresh blueberries, optional

Combine ice cream and yogurt in large bowl; blend well. Gradually add bourbon and nutmeg. Spread filling evenly inside meringue; cover with an overturned bowl; freeze 4 hours or overnight. Shortly before serving, whip cream with confectioners' sugar; spread over top of pie or pipe on with pastry bag and tube. Cut pie into small wedges; serve with blueberries, if desired.

Strawberry Yogurt Pie

Makes 1 9-inch pie.

- 2 8-ounce containers strawberry yogurt
- 1 8- or 9-ounce container whipped topping, thawed
- 1 pint sliced strawberries
- 1 teaspoon vanilla
- 1 9-inch graham cracker crust

Combine yogurt and whipped topping in large bowl. Add ⅔ of strawberries and vanilla; stir gently. Spoon into crust. Garnish with remaining sliced strawberries; freeze at least 4 hours. Remove from freezer and place in refrigerator 30 minutes before serving. Store any leftover pie in freezer.

Frosty Piña Colada Yogurt Pie

Makes 1 8-inch pie.

- 1 8¼-ounce can crushed pineapple, including liquid
- 2 8-ounce containers piña colada yogurt
- ½ cup whipping cream
- 3 tablespoons honey
- 1 cup (24 to 30 cookies) vanilla wafer crumbs
- ½ cup flaked coconut
- ⅓ cup butter or margarine, melted
  Coconut for garnish
  Lime slices for garnish

Pour pineapple, including liquid, into small saucepan; boil rapidly until syrup is reduced and mixture is almost dry. Watch closely to prevent scorching; cool. Combine pineapple and yogurt in bowl. Blend well. Beat cream with honey just until stiff. Fold into yogurt mixture. Turn into shallow pan; place in freezer while preparing crust. Combine vanilla wafer crumbs, coconut and melted butter until thoroughly blended. Press mixture against bottom and sides of 8-inch pie plate. Bake at 350° 10 minutes, until lightly browned; cool. After filling has chilled sufficiently to hold its shape, remove and spoon into cooled shell. Return pie to freezer until completely frozen. Garnish with additional coconut and lime slices. Let stand in refrigerator 10 to 15 minutes before cutting.

Frozen Brandy Alexander Pie

Makes 1 9-inch pie.

- 2 pints coffee ice cream, softened
- 1 8-ounce container frozen vanilla yogurt, softened
- ¼ cup creme de cacao
- 3 tablespoons brandy
- 1 baked 9-inch meringue shell
- 1 cup heavy cream
- 2 tablespoons confectioners' sugar
- 1 1-ounce square bittersweet chocolate

Combine ice cream and yogurt in large bowl; blend well. Gradually add creme de cacao and brandy; mix thoroughly. Spread filling evenly inside meringue, cover with an overturned bowl and freeze 4 hours or overnight. Shortly before serving, whip cream with confectioners' sugar; spread over top of pie or pipe on with pastry bag and tube. Shave chocolate with vegetable peeler and sprinkle over pie.

Surprise Chocolate Pie

Makes 1 9-inch pie.

Crust

- 2½ cups flaked coconut
- ¼ cup butter, melted

Preheat oven to 350°. Toss coconut with butter until evenly coated. Press onto bottom and sides of 9-inch pie pan. Bake 15 to 20 minutes or until lightly browned; cool.

Filling

- 1 6-ounce package chocolate pudding and pie filling mix
- 1¾ cups milk
- 1 8-ounce container coffee yogurt
  Whipped cream
  Chocolate curls

Combine pudding mix and milk in saucepan; bring to boil over medium heat, stirring constantly. Boil and stir 1 minute; remove from heat. Stir in yogurt. Pour into crust. Chill 6 hours or overnight. Garnish with whipped cream and chocolate curls.

Pies

Lemon-Lime Chiffon Pie

Makes 1 9-inch pie.

Crust

1½ cups graham cracker crumbs
2 tablespoons granulated sugar
⅓ cup melted butter

Preheat oven to 375°. Combine crumbs, sugar and butter in bowl; firmly press mixture onto bottom and sides of 9-inch pie pan. Bake 8 to 10 minutes or until lightly browned. Cool completely before filling.

Filling

1 envelope unflavored gelatin
1 cup granulated sugar
¼ teaspoon salt
3 eggs, separated
⅓ cup water
2 teaspoons grated lime rind
⅓ cup fresh lime juice
1 8-ounce container lemon yogurt

Combine gelatin, ¾ cup sugar and salt in top of double boiler. Blend in egg yolks, water, lime rind and juice. Cook over simmering water, stirring constantly, until mixture thickens and coats a spoon, about 10 minutes. Chill until mixture mounds when spooned, 30 to 45 minutes. Fold in yogurt. Beat egg whites until foamy in bowl; gradually add ¼ cup sugar and beat until stiff. Fold into gelatin mixture. Pour into cooled piecrust. Chill at least 3 hours.

Yogurt Pumpkin Pie

Makes 1 9-inch pie.

Sesame Crust
2 eggs
½ cup firmly packed brown sugar
½ cup granulated sugar
½ teaspoon salt
1 teaspoon cinnamon
½ teaspoon ginger
¼ teaspoon ground nutmeg
⅓ teaspoon allspice
¼ teaspoon grated lemon rind
¼ teaspoon grated orange rind
1 8-ounce container plain yogurt
⅔ cup evaporated milk or half-and-half
1 1-pound can pumpkin
Sweetened whipped cream
1 teaspoon toasted sesame seeds for garnish

Prepare Sesame Crust; set aside. Preheat oven to 400°. Beat eggs well; add sugars, salt, cinnamon, ginger, nutmeg, allspice and lemon and orange rind. Stir in yogurt, milk and pumpkin. Pour into prepared crust. Bake in lower third of oven for 45 minutes or until barely set in center. Remove to wire rack to cool. When ready to serve, top with mounds of sweetened whipped cream and sprinkle with sesame seeds.

Sesame Crust

1½ cups sifted flour
¾ teaspoon salt
½ cup shortening
2 tablespoons toasted sesame seeds
¼ cup cold water, approximately

Sift flour and salt together in bowl. Cut in shortening; stir in sesame seeds. Add enough water to hold pastry together. Shape pastry into ball; roll out on floured surface. Line 9-inch pie pan, making a high fluted rim.

Apricot Fluff Pie

Makes 1 9-inch pie.

Crust

2 cups finely crushed crisp rice cereal
¼ cup honey
¼ cup butter or margarine, melted

Preheat oven to 350°. Combine all ingredients; mix well. Press onto bottom and sides of buttered 9-inch pie plate. Bake 8 to 10 minutes. Cool.

Filling

1 16-ounce can apricot halves
2 envelopes unflavored gelatin
2 8-ounce containers apricot yogurt
¼ cup honey
⅛ teaspoon salt
1 cup whipping cream

Drain apricots, reserving ½ cup liquid. Soften gelatin in reserved liquid. Dissolve gelatin mixture over low heat in small saucepan; cool. Combine apricots, yogurt, honey and salt in food processor or blender. Process until apricots are chopped. Add dissolved gelatin; blend well. Pour mixture into large bowl. Chill until thick. Beat whipping cream until thickened and fold into apricot mixture. Pour into prepared Crust. Chill several hours before serving.

Fruited Creme Fraiche

Makes 4 servings.

- 2 medium nectarines *or* peaches, peeled and sliced
- 1 8-ounce container plain yogurt
  Few drops almond extract
  Honey *or* granulated sugar, to taste
- 1 envelope unflavored gelatin
- 2 tablespoons water
  Nectarine slices for garnish
  Mint sprigs for garnish

Combine nectarines, yogurt and almond extract in blender. Blend until smooth. Add honey or sugar to taste. Combine gelatin and water in small saucepan; stir over low heat until dissolved. Add to mixture in blender; blend 10 seconds. Chill until mixture begins to thicken. Spoon into stemmed glasses and chill until set. Garnish with additional nectarine slices and mint sprigs.

Berries 'n' Cream Dessert

Makes 4 servings.

- 2 envelopes unflavored gelatin
- ⅔ cup granulated sugar
- 3 eggs, separated
- 1 cup milk
- 2 8-ounce containers red raspberry, strawberry *or* boysenberry yogurt
- 1 cup heavy cream, whipped

Combine gelatin and ⅓ cup sugar in medium saucepan. Beat egg yolks with milk; blend egg yolk mixture into gelatin mixture. Stir over low heat until gelatin dissolves, about 5 minutes. Blend in yogurt with wire whisk; chill, stirring frequently, until mixture mounds slightly when dropped from spoon. Beat egg whites in medium bowl until soft peaks form. Gradually add remaining ⅓ cup sugar and beat until stiff. Fold in gelatin mixture, then whipped cream. Spoon into individual glasses; chill until set.

Apple Dessert Parfaits

Makes 2 servings.

- 1 8-ounce container vanilla yogurt
- 1 8-ounce container apple yogurt
- ½ cup slivered toasted almonds
- ½ cup raisins
  Maple syrup *or* sugar to taste
  Nutmeg, if desired

Combine all ingredients in bowl; chill. Spoon chilled mixture into parfait glasses and serve.

Vanilla Mold with Cherries

Makes 4 servings.

- 1 envelope unflavored gelatin
- ⅛ teaspoon salt
- ¼ cup water
- 2 8-ounce containers vanilla yogurt
- 1½ cups sweet cherries

Combine gelatin, salt and water in saucepan. Heat until dissolved. Remove from heat; stir in yogurt. Blend well. Turn into 3-cup mold. Chill until set. Unmold and serve with cherries.

Honey Yogurt Sundae

Makes 1 serving.

- 1 8-ounce container plain yogurt
- 2 tablespoons honey
- 2 tablespoons chopped almonds
- 2 tablespoons chopped dates

Spoon yogurt into chilled dish. Pour honey over yogurt; sprinkle with almonds and dates.

Fluffy Coffee Mousse

Makes 4 servings.

- 1 envelope unflavored gelatin
- ¼ cup cold water
- ¾ cup boiling water
- 1 tablespoon instant espresso powder
- 1 egg white, beaten
- 1 8-ounce container coffee yogurt
- 1 tablespoon granulated sugar
- ½ teaspoon ground cinnamon
  Whipped cream for garnish, optional
- 4 coffee beans, optional

Soften gelatin in cold water in small bowl. Add boiling water; stir until gelatin dissolves. Add instant espresso powder. Chill until mixture is slightly thickened. Add egg white to gelatin mixture; place bowl in ice water in a second bowl. Beat at high speed with electric mixer until soft peaks form. Fold in yogurt, sugar and cinnamon. Wrap aluminum foil around 4 after-dinner or demitasse cups and secure with paper clips to make a collar. Fill cups with yogurt mixture. Refrigerate at least 2 hours or until set. Carefully peel off foil. Garnish with a dollop of whipped cream and 1 coffee bean, if desired.

Red Raspberry Mousse

Makes 4 servings.

- 2 egg whites, stiffly beaten
- ½ cup heavy cream, whipped
- 2 tablespoons rum
- 2 8-ounce containers red raspberry yogurt *or* any fruit yogurt desired
- 1 cup toasted coconut
- 2 tablespoons grated orange rind

Fold egg whites into whipped cream in large bowl. Stir in rum and yogurt. Blend in coconut and orange rind. Spoon into serving bowl or individual glasses; freeze until firm, but not solid.

Frozen Bananas

Makes 10.

- 1 8-ounce container plain yogurt
- ¼ cup honey
- 5 firm bananas
- 1 cup flaked coconut, toasted *or* chopped almonds, toasted

Blend yogurt and honey in small bowl. Peel bananas; cut in half crosswise and insert a flat wooden stick into cut end of each half. Dip banana halves in yogurt mixture to coat completely; set aside remaining yogurt mixture. Place bananas slightly apart on baking sheet lined with waxed paper. Cover with plastic wrap; freeze 1 hour. When coating on bananas is firm, dip each banana in yogurt mixture again; roll in coconut or almonds. Return to baking sheet, cover and freeze. Before serving, thaw about 5 minutes.

Note: Will keep 2 weeks in freezer.

Variation

Fruit-Flavored Yogurt Bananas: Follow directions above, except omit plain yogurt and honey; substitute 1 cup well-blended fruit yogurt.

Fruit 'n' Honey Celebration

Makes 6 servings.

- 2 envelopes unflavored gelatin
- 1½ cups orange juice
- 2 8-ounce containers plain, vanilla *or* lemon yogurt
- 1 11-ounce can mandarin oranges, drained, reserve liquid
- 2 tablespoons honey
- ½ cup raisins
- ½ cup chopped walnuts
- 2 bananas, cut into ½-inch slices

Sprinkle gelatin over 1 cup orange juice in medium saucepan. Stir over low heat until gelatin dissolves, about 3 minutes. Blend in yogurt, remaining orange juice, reserved liquid and honey with wire whisk. Chill, stirring frequently, until mixture is slightly thickened. Fold in oranges, raisins, walnuts and bananas. Turn into 6-cup mold or individual dessert dishes; chill until firm, about 3 hours.

Frozen Lemon Yogurt Soufflé

- 2 16-ounce containers plain yogurt
- 1 cup granulated sugar
- Juice and finely grated rind of 2 lemons
- 1 teaspoon vanilla extract
- Pinch cream of tartar
- Pinch salt
- 2 egg whites
- ½ cup heavy cream, whipped
- Lemon slices for garnish

Combine yogurt and sugar in bowl; add lemon juice, rind and vanilla; blend well. Add cream of tartar and salt to egg whites in bowl; beat until stiff. Gently fold egg whites into yogurt mixture; fold in whipped cream. Place in 4-cup soufflé dish; freeze overnight. Garnish with lemon slices.

Baked Custard

Makes 6 servings.

- 4 eggs
- 1 8-ounce container fruit yogurt
- ⅓ cup granulated sugar
- 2 tablespoons flour
- ¼ teaspoon salt
- 2 cups hot milk
- 1 teaspoon vanilla
- Nutmeg, optional

Preheat oven to 350°. Blend eggs, yogurt, sugar, flour and salt together in large bowl. Gradually stir in milk. Blend in vanilla. Pour into six 6-ounce custard cups or 1½-quart shallow casserole. Sprinkle with nutmeg, if desired. Set custard cups or casserole in large baking pan; place pan in oven. Pour hot water into pan to within ½-inch of top of custard. Bake 30 to 35 minutes for cups or 35 to 40 minutes for casserole or until knife inserted near center comes out clean. Remove immediately from hot water. Serve warm or chilled.

Frozen Yogurt

Frozen Cherry Almond Yogurt

Makes 1½ quarts.

    1 envelope unflavored gelatin
    ½ cup granulated sugar
    ¼ cup cold water
    1 32-ounce container plain yogurt
    2 teaspoons almond extract
    1 pound fresh cherries, pitted and halved
    1 cup chopped toasted almonds

Combine gelatin, sugar and water in small saucepan; stir over low heat until gelatin dissolves. Stir in 1 cup yogurt. Transfer gelatin mixture to large bowl; stir in remaining ingredients. Pour into ice cream freezer; freeze according to manufacturer's directions. Soft-frozen yogurt can be served at once or transferred to freezer container, covered and frozen at least 2 hours or longer to develop flavors.

Frozen Peach Yogurt

Makes 1½ quarts.

    1 envelope unflavored gelatin
    ¼ cup cold water
  1½ cups sliced peaches, fresh *or* frozen,
       partially thawed
    ⅓ cup granulated sugar
    4 8-ounce containers peach yogurt
      Orange Raspberry Sauce
      Sliced peaches, optional

Sprinkle gelatin over water in small saucepan; stir over low heat until dissolved. Puree peaches with sugar in blender; add yogurt and blend at high speed until smooth. Stir 1 cup yogurt mixture into dissolved gelatin; return to blender, cover and blend until smooth. Fill ice cream freezer two-thirds full. Freeze according to manufacturer's directions. Serve with Orange Raspberry Sauce and additional sliced fresh peaches, if desired.

Orange Raspberry Sauce

Makes 1½ cups.

    1 10-ounce package frozen raspberries in
       syrup, thawed
    ⅓ cup orange marmalade
    1 tablespoon cornstarch
    2 tablespoons water

Heat raspberries and marmalade in saucepan over medium heat; *do not boil.* Dissolve cornstarch in water; add to fruit mixture and stir until thickened.

Fresh Plum Frozen Yogurt

Makes approximately 1 quart.

    3 cups pitted and quartered fresh plums
    1 8-ounce container plain yogurt
    ½ cup light corn syrup
    ¼ to ½ cup granulated sugar
    ¼ teaspoon almond extract
    ¼ teaspoon vanilla
      Pinch salt

Spread plums on a cookie sheet. Freeze firm; store in covered containers. Blend all remaining ingredients for 30 seconds in blender. (For tart frozen yogurt use ¼ cup sugar; add more sugar for sweeter taste.) With blender on high speed, drop plums, 1 or 2 pieces at a time, through opening in lid; blend smooth. Serve immediately or freeze until slushy, stirring occasionally, or freeze firm.

Blueberry Frozen Yogurt

Makes 1 quart.

    1 tablespoon unflavored gelatin
    2 tablespoons cold water
    2 tablespoons boiling water
    2 8-ounce containers plain yogurt
    1 cup fresh blueberries
    ⅓ cup nonfat powdered milk
    ¼ to ⅓ cup honey, to taste

Soften gelatin in cold water in bowl. Add boiling water and stir until gelatin is dissolved. Place gelatin and all remaining ingredients in blender; blend until smooth. Pour into ice cream freezer; freeze according to manufacturer's directions.

Variation: Strawberries, raspberries, peaches or apricots may be substituted for blueberries. If using raspberries, puree first in blender, then strain and discard seeds.

Frozen Chocolate Yogurt

Makes 1½ pints.

    2 8-ounce containers vanilla yogurt
    1 cup cocoa powder
    1 cup confectioners' sugar
    1 envelope unflavored gelatin
    ¼ cup lukewarm water

Combine yogurt, cocoa powder and sugar in blender. Dissolve gelatin in water; add to yogurt mixture and blend until smooth. Pour into ice cream maker. Freeze according to manufacturer's directions.

Soft-Frozen Raspberry Dessert

Makes approximately 1 quart.

- **1 envelope unflavored gelatin**
- **¼ cup cold water**
- **1 10-ounce package frozen raspberries, thawed**
- **3 8-ounce containers plain yogurt**

Sprinkle gelatin over water in small saucepan; set aside 5 minutes to soften. Cook over low heat, stirring constantly, until gelatin is completely dissolved. Strain raspberries, discarding seeds. Pour dissolved gelatin into large bowl. Blend in yogurt, 1 container at a time; stir in raspberries. Pour mixture into 9-inch square baking pan; freeze, stirring several times, about 3 hours or until slushy. Place mixture into chilled bowl. Beat with electric mixer until smooth. For soft-frozen yogurt, place in freezer 30 minutes. Yogurt will freeze solid if left in freezer more than 30 minutes.

Variation

Soft-Frozen Strawberry Yogurt: Substitute 1 10-ounce package frozen strawberries partially thawed and pureed for the raspberries.

Soft-Frozen Peach Yogurt: Substitute 1 10-ounce package frozen peaches partially thawed and pureed in blender and ¼ teaspoon almond flavoring, for the raspberries.

Frozen Piña Colada Yogurt

Makes approximately 1 quart.

- **1 envelope unflavored gelatin**
- **¼ cup water**
- **1 8¼-ounce can crushed pineapple in juice**
- **8 ounces cream of coconut**
- **2 8-ounce containers plain yogurt**
- **2 tablespoons rum**
- **2 egg whites**
- **3 tablespoons granulated sugar**
- **Pineapple wedges, optional**
- **Toasted coconut, optional**

Sprinkle gelatin over water in small saucepan; set aside 5 minutes to soften. Cook over low heat, stirring constantly. Place undrained pineapple in blender; blend on medium speed until smooth. Blend in cream of coconut, yogurt, rum and gelatin mixture. Pour into a 9-inch square baking pan. Freeze, stirring occasionally, until partially frozen, 2 to 3 hours. Beat egg whites until foamy and double in volume in small bowl. Beat in sugar, 1 tablespoon at a time, until meringue forms soft peaks. Spoon partially frozen mixture into chilled large bowl. Beat with electric mixer until smooth. Fold in meringue quickly. Spoon into bowl; freeze 2 hours. Spoon into individual serving dishes. Garnish with a pineapple wedge and toasted coconut, if desired.

Frozen Pineapple Sherbet

Makes 1 quart.

- **1 envelope unflavored gelatin**
- **¾ cup granulated sugar**
- **½ cup pineapple juice**
- **2 8-ounce containers plain yogurt**
- **2 tablespoons lemon *or* orange juice**

Combine gelatin and sugar in 1-quart saucepan. Stir in pineapple juice; cook over low heat, stirring, until gelatin is completely dissolved. Remove from heat; stir in yogurt and lemon juice. Pour into freezer container. Cover and freeze until firm. To serve, let sherbet stand at room temperature 20 minutes for easier serving.

Vanilla Frozen Yogurt

Makes 1 quart.

- **¾ cup granulated sugar**
- **1 envelope unflavored gelatin**
- **Pinch salt**
- **1 cup milk**
- **2½ cups plain yogurt**
- **1 tablespoon vanilla extract**

Combine sugar, gelatin and salt in small saucepan. Add milk; cook over low heat at least 5 minutes, stirring constantly, until gelatin and sugar are thoroughly dissolved. Remove from heat; cool to room temperature. Blend in yogurt and vanilla. Cover; refrigerate until cool.* Pour mixture into 4-quart ice cream maker freezer container. Freeze according to manufacturer's directions. Let stand 2 to 3 hours in freezer prior to serving.

*May be prepared in advance to this point and kept refrigerated up to 24 hours.

Lemon Frost

Makes 6 servings.

½ **envelope unflavored gelatin**
¼ **cup water**
1 **cup milk**
2 **8-ounce containers lemon yogurt**
2 **teaspoons lemon juice**
¼ **teaspoon vanilla**

Sprinkle gelatin over water in saucepan; mix well. Add milk, yogurt, lemon juice and vanilla to gelatin mixture; beat with wire whisk. Heat over medium heat until gelatin is dissolved. Pour into ice cream freezer and follow manufacturer's directions or pour into serving bowl and freeze about 4 hours.

Maple Walnut Frozen Yogurt

Makes 1½ pints.

½ **cup evaporated milk**
¼ **cup maple syrup**
2 **8-ounce containers plain yogurt**
½ **cup chopped walnuts**

Scald milk over low heat, stirring occasionally. Add maple syrup; cool. Combine milk mixture, yogurt and nuts in blender or food processor. Pour into ice cream maker; freeze according to manufacturer's directions.

Frozen Strawberry Yogurt

Makes approximately 1½ quarts.

1 **envelope unflavored gelatin**
¼ **cup orange juice**
½ **cup grenadine**
1 **pint fresh strawberries, washed and hulled** or
2 **cups unsweetened frozen strawberries**
2 **8-ounce containers plain yogurt**
½ **cup sour cream**
2 **egg whites**
¼ **cup granulated sugar**

Sprinkle gelatin over orange juice in small saucepan; set aside 5 minutes to soften. Cook over low heat until gelatin is dissolved; cool. Combine grenadine, strawberries, yogurt and sour cream in blender; blend on medium speed until smooth. Blend in gelatin mixture. Pour into a 9-inch square baking pan. Place in freezer, stirring occasionally, until partially frozen, 2 to 3 hours. Beat egg whites until foamy and double in volume in small bowl. Beat in sugar, 1 tablespoon at a time, until meringue forms soft peaks. Spoon

Clockwise from top:
Frozen Peach Yogurt, page 60
Frozen Chocolate Yogurt, page 60
Frozen Cherry-Almond Yogurt, page 60
Maple-Walnut Frozen Yogurt
Blueberry Frozen Yogurt, page 60

partially frozen mixture into chilled large bowl. Beat with electric mixer until smooth. Fold in meringue quickly. Spoon into freezer container or bowl. Freeze about 2 hours for soft-frozen yogurt, or freeze solid and remove from freezer 15 to 30 minutes prior to serving.

Orange Yogurt Sherbet

Makes approximately 2 quarts.

1 **envelope unflavored gelatin**
2 **cups orange juice**
1 **cup granulated sugar**
¼ **teaspoon salt**
2 **teaspoons grated orange rind**
½ **cup flaked coconut**
2 **8-ounce containers plain yogurt**

Sprinkle gelatin over ½ cup orange juice in medium saucepan over low heat. Stir constantly until gelatin dissolves, about 3 minutes. Add sugar and salt; stir until sugar dissolves. Remove from heat; stir in remaining orange juice, orange rind and coconut. Cool slightly; blend in yogurt. Freeze mixture in a 2- or 4-quart ice cream maker according to manufacturer's directions. Place in bowl, cover and freeze about 2 hours.

Banana Frozen Yogurt

Makes approximately 1½ quarts.

1 **envelope unflavored gelatin**
¼ **cup cold water** or **orange juice**
½ **cup granulated sugar**
¼ **teaspoon salt**
1 **cup mashed bananas**
1 **tablespoon lemon juice**
1 **8-ounce container plain yogurt**
2 **egg whites**

Sprinkle gelatin over water in small saucepan; cook over low heat, stirring constantly, until gelatin dissolves, about 3 minutes. Stir in sugar and salt. Remove from heat. Blend in bananas and lemon juice. Stir in yogurt. Pour into freezer tray or 9 x 5 x 3-inch loaf pan. Freeze until firm. Turn mixture into large bowl; add egg whites. Beat at high speed until smooth and fluffy, about 10 minutes. Return to freezer tray; freeze until firm.

Variation

Banana-Rum-Raisin Frozen Yogurt: Substitute 2 tablespoons rum *or* 1 teaspoon rum flavoring for lemon juice in basic recipe. Fold in ½ cup raisins after beating banana yogurt with egg whites. Return to freezer tray; freeze until firm.

Index